GW00337615

Supplement

Issue No. 1

Supplement's first ever cover comes in two iterations. The first features French/English actor **Stacy Martin** wearing **Miu Miu**, shot in London by **Mark Peckmezian** and styled by **Ellie Grace Cumming**. The second features an exclusive shoot by **Albert Watson** of model **Lou Schoof** wearing **Dries Van Noten**, styled by **Paul Sinclaire** in New York

Joint Editors-in-Chief/Creative Direction
Tom Lardner & Chris West

Art Direction/Design
Callum Walker

Designer
Marcin Liwarski

Joint Editors
Justin Quirk
Alex Rayner

Sub-Editor
Vanessa Harriss

Senior Marketing Executive
Rhiannon Welfare

Production
Plus Agency
plusagency.co.uk

Publishers
Tom Lardner & Chris West

Printing
Leycol
leycol.com

Paper
Munken Design by G.F Smith
Lynx Smooth Natural White
gfsmith.com

Typefaces
Centaur MT & Classic Grotesque
both by Monotype
monotype.com

UK Distribution
MMS Limited
mmslondon.co.uk

International Distribution
Export Press
exportpress.com

Contributing Writers
Cath Clarke
Lauren Cochrane
Dylan Kerr
Justin Quirk
Alex Rayner
Amei Wallach

Contributing Photographers
Jeff Boudreau
Lasse Fløde
Paul Maffi
Rory Payne
Mark Peckmezian
Daniel Shea
Rory van Millingen
Albert Watson

Contributing Stylists
Ellie Grace Cumming
Andrew Davis
Cristina Holmes
Verity Parker
Victoria Sekrier
Paul Sinclaire

Contributing Illustrator
Rune Fisker

Special Thanks
Katy Barker, Justine Bayley, Sophie Castley, Robert Diament,
Sinead Foley, James Fooks-Bale, John Haslam, Walker Hinerman,
Laura Holmes, Lucy Lehane, Alec Mather, Amelia Redgrift,
Sandra Rose, Margaret Sweeney, Birgitta Toyoda, Molly Wansell,
Chantelle Webber, Gary Wilson. Extra special thanks to Steven Layton

Supplement is published twice yearly by Plus Agency,
2nd Floor, 53a Brewer Street, London, W1F 9UH
Printed in London, UK. ISBN 978-0-9934142-0-6

supplementmagazine.co.uk
contact@supplementmagazine.co.uk
Instagram: @supplement_mag

Contents

Contributors

Albert Watson – Photographer

Albert Watson was born in
Edinburgh in 1942 and began his
photographic career in the US
during the 1970s. He has shot
covers for the likes of American
Vogue and *Rolling Stone*, and was
awarded an OBE in 2015 in the
Queen's Birthday Honours list.
His shoot appears on *page 66*

Amei Wallach – Writer

Amei Wallach is an art critic,
filmmaker and author. Her articles
have appeared in such publications
as *The New York Times Magazine*,
Vanity Fair and *The Brooklyn Rail*.
She was also chief art critic for
New York *Newsday*. Her profile
of the artist Rashid Johnson
appears on *page 16*

Mark Peckmezian – Photographer

Mark Peckmezian graduated in
2010 and released his first book,
Photographs & Pictures, the same
year. He won Portrait of the Year
at Canada's National Magazine
Awards and has shot for *AnOther*,
Vogue Hommes, *M Le Monde*, and
The Gentlewoman. His story
appears on *page 44*

Paul Sinclaire – Stylist

Fashion editor Paul Sinclaire has
worked at American *Vogue*, *L'Uomo
Vogue*, *i-D* and *The Face*, and with
photographers such as Steven Klein
and Nathaniel Goldberg. His work
has appeared in *Hero* and *Arena
HOMME+* and his shoot,
featuring Dries Van Noten's
new collection, is on *page 66*

Rune Fisker – Illustrator

Growing up in Denmark, Rune
spent most of his time drawing
with and on anything. Now he runs
his own animation company Benny
Box. Rune's abstract, surrealist style
plays with geometries, line and
tone. Rune's distorted characters
appear alongside an interview with
Will Davies on *page 37*

Victoria Sekrier – Stylist

Victoria Sekrier is a Russian
stylist based in London who
moved into the more creative
realms of the fashion world after
10 years as a model. She divides
her time between shooting editorial
projects and styling the acclaimed
Swedish actress Alicia Vikander.
Her story appears on *page 26*

Foreword

Supplement is a new magazine devoted to contemporary culture in its widest sense. We hope to draw connections between the art produced in the margins of society and the simple, everyday way in which people change and reimagine their own lives; between the old avant-garde and the new frontiers of experimentation; between beautifully crafted images and long-form writing.

Rashid Johnson works through the perils of African-American fatherhood with his heavily incised updates of Edvard Munch's *The Scream*; Kenneth Goldsmith rebuilds 20th century New York from mountains of citations and discarded lines; Stacy Martin, having survived a lead role in Lars von Trier's *Nymphomaniac*, plays the perfect fall girl in the new film adaptation of JG Ballard's *High-Rise*. Albert Watson introduces his *Children of the Coal*; Rory Payne takes us back to Georgia O'Keeffe's Ghost Ranch and Rory van Millingen experiments with contemporary colour and shape. Meanwhile, Paul Maffi spends some time with model Tilda Lindstam and Lasse Fløde shoots a selection of this season's finest brooches.

This issue also features work of Deborah Turbeville, David Bailey, Bruce Rogers and Katherine Bernhardt. Within the pages of *Supplement* suburban bodybuilders rub shoulders with primitive art, modern jewellery and the political quest for happiness. It's a big world out there. We think there's room in our lives to draw inspiration from all this, and we hope to capture that excitement in this and forthcoming issues of the magazine.

Hooked on Bailey

Words by Alex Rayner

Why is a revered European gallery taking torn photographs and fish hooks to Frieze?

"281 Society Island, c." Courtesy of Daniel Blau

Can an artwork be useful, or does usefulness prevent it from being true art? Is all art, as Oscar Wilde once wrote, "quite useless"? And, if rendered useless once more, might an object contend for artistic status? Perhaps these thoughts will cross the minds of visitors this October when they look at the works on show at Daniel Blau's Frieze Masters stand.

The Munich gallery is taking part in a new section at the art fair called Collections. Overseen by Sir Norman Rosenthal, the Royal Academy's former head of exhibitions, Collections will show eight presentations that, the fair says, "contain within them germs of ideas for exhibitions that could easily take place at any of the great public institutions in the world." Blau will present a collection of fish hooks and torn photographs. The hooks are traditional, hand-made items from the Pacific islands and, in some cases, date back to antiquity. The photographs are 20th century, from David Bailey's personal archive, and were test prints, produced on scraps of photographic paper, prior to printing a full-scale image.

"In the darkroom you used to use scraps to check the exposure time is correct," Blau explains. "Bailey kept boxes and boxes of these fragments. I really like them. Even if the photograph isn't so very interesting, the torn version of a portrait can be quite exciting because there's an element of chance, since the paper is ripped before they're ripped, before they're exposed." Blau, son of the German post-war painter Georg Baselitz,

is better known for his exhibitions of contemporary art and photography, although he cultivates a wide range of esoteric interests. The gallerist came across the hooks in Hawaii while he was photographing the island's petroglyphs back in the 1980s. "You could find these lying around," he recalls. "The first people came from Hawaii about 1,500 years ago, and the oldest hooks date from that time."

He acknowledges that the hooks served a function, one that was utterly vital to the lives of Pacific islanders. "They had nothing but coral, sand and bushes and still people had to make a living," he explains. "This is not a simple tool like a nail and a hammer. They are central to the society, and so adored and venerated and quite valuable." It is perhaps better to think of them in the same way that we regard medals in the West, Blau argues. He says that, although some of the hooks are a little hard to appreciate, many of his artistic friends admire and enjoy this interest of his. He has even published a highly regarded book, *Fish Hooks of the Pacific Islands*. "It's the fish-hook bible," he laughs.

Will the international art collectors gathering in London this autumn share this enthusiasm? Both these torn prints and these fishing implements were once useful objects, tools in a sense, though neither seem limited to this status. "They have outgrown that," says Blau, "and they have become something else." *danielblau.com*

Uncharted – Mick Jagger, 1970
© David Bailey
Courtesy of Daniel Blau

Badges of distinction

Words by Lauren Cochrane
Photography by Lasse Fløde / Styling by Cristina Holmes

What do we picture when we think of rock'n'roll jewellery? Nose piercings perhaps, or a cacophony of earrings up the wearer's lobe, mixed with tattoos and eyeliner and a choker around the neck; a cluster of chunky silver rings from Chrome Hearts, as worn by Karl Lagerfeld with black fingerless gloves; trashy hoop earrings such as those worn by Cyndi Lauper and Madonna in the 80s, with bangles up to the elbow. Certainly not a brooch.

Nevertheless, the humble brooch — more usually found on your grandmother's lapel than on catwalk models — has been rediscovered. Chanel, Céline, Loewe and Balenciaga have all featured them. In the case of Balenciaga, models wore lots of jewellery, trad brooches included. The initials of the founder, Cristóbal Balenciaga, were rendered in diamanté and, with a tiny sceptre worthy of the Queen, pinned on delicately cut checked coats. On paper, this might read like conservative dressing circa 1963, yet

> ## "Fashion has rediscovered a love for slightly fusty things that look a bit anachronistic in a world of bright, shiny screens"

it was given a twist by the 31-year-old American designer Alexander Wang. In his world, brooches still have that ladylike aspect; however, when they're combined with ear cuffs, flat chunky boots and, in the case of most models, a scowl, they looked almost subversive.

This juxtaposition of old-fashioned and modern modes of dressing — a neat trick that suits fashion now — has brought back the brooch in a way that those under the retirement age can connect with. The brooch's newfound place is part of a wider trend, a rediscovery of the jewellery box, as it were. Once an afterthought, jewellery is taking the place of handbags as the kicker of any outfit, the one piece that defines how a woman wants to be perceived. Céline demonstrated this effect with the humble hair clip last season. The round gold pins worn in the hair of models became a much-imitated cult item.

Now brooches are occupying a similar position. On the catwalk they were often worn in slightly odd places or made from odd materials. It's this off-kilter thing that makes it work, making them less Barbara Cartland and more Little Edie from *Grey Gardens*. See Dolce & Gabbana and Prada, where jewelled brooches were worn in the models' hair, or Céline, where they were clipped onto shoes, in one of those trademark touches of Phoebe Philo wonkiness. Plenty of Prada's dresses came with either the kind of classic sparkly brooches that are familiar from rootling around in elderly relatives' jewellery boxes, or oversized Perspex flowers in primary brights. They all clashed — in a Miuccia-approved sickly-sweet way — with the pastel mid-century shades of the clothes.

Givenchy, meanwhile, arguably got the prize for weirdest use of brooches. In a collection that fused the unlikely inspirations of Mexican chola culture with Victorian jet jewellery, models sported brooch-like sparkles on their cheeks, paired with giant nose rings and long, gothic gowns. It's a long way from a sparkly thistle to brighten up a sensible coat.

Fashion is all about status, and brooches have always been status symbols, as evinced by stateswomen ranging from Jackie Kennedy to Grace Kelly and Margaret Thatcher. This may be because the brooch is one of the oldest jewellery items recorded, worn by the wealthy, sometimes with script that denoted the high-ranking position of the wearer. The brooch dates back to the Roman era and was originally known as a fibula, similar in shape to a safety pin but more decorative. Celtic tradition saw the rise of the penannular brooch, which came with ring design and elegant filigree. Then there's the cameo, the 19th century style favoured by Queen Victoria and worn by many of her subjects at the throat of a leg-o-mutton blouse. It was also sometimes combined with the excellently named stomacher, worn on the middle of a dress.

While stomachers are no longer in fashion, surely the revival is only a matter of time. For the last five years everything has been about the clean, the slick and the discreetly expensive, but now fashion has rediscovered a love for slightly fusty things that look a bit anachronistic in a world of bright, shiny screens. Something that might have been found in a shortbread tin at a car-boot sale is suddenly stylish. There's a vintage feel in fashion, one that isn't connected to a particular era or about referencing any specific style icon. Instead, it's a sort of pick'n'mix approach to what we wear, one that reflects the random nature of what you find when shopping secondhand. The brooch, the epitome of a knick-knack, is an easy way to pin that trend onto modern clothing, to add something odd to an otherwise anonymous wardrobe; and make it odder still if pinned in an unusual place. Man Repeller's Leandra Medine, the internet's patron saint of kooky fashion and a latter-day Little Edie, wears hers on a belt, or halfway up a sleeve.

And yet the brooch is conservative, it's proper, it's respectable — that's why the Queen wears them. Most of her public engagements this year, from a WI meeting to her granddaughter's christening, saw her brooched-up and resplendent in pastels. But fashion isn't holding her up as a style icon for the brooch trend. Instead, as Medine demonstrates, this is sort of about taking that and twisting it, making it into something odd, something One might not approve of. That works precisely because it's the same thing that One might wear, but in a very different way. With the brooch, fashion is enjoying a moment of rebellion. It really is the most rock'n'roll thing you can wear this season. Just don't tell your grandmother.

Right: Black mesh top, American Apparel
Black mesh gloves, Vintage
Black lattice jumpsuit, Natasha Zinko
Crystal fern brooch, Balenciaga

Left: Black sleeveless dress, Solace
Silver safety-pin brooch, Givenchy

Right: Black net long-sleeve body, Julien McDonald
Black wide-leg cropped trousers, Roksanda Illincic
Gold bow brooch, Dolce & Gabbana

Left: Black ribbed patent leather body, Jitrois
Silver Meccano pin, Loewe

Right: Long black leather coat, Jitrois
Crystal spider brooch, Saint Laurent

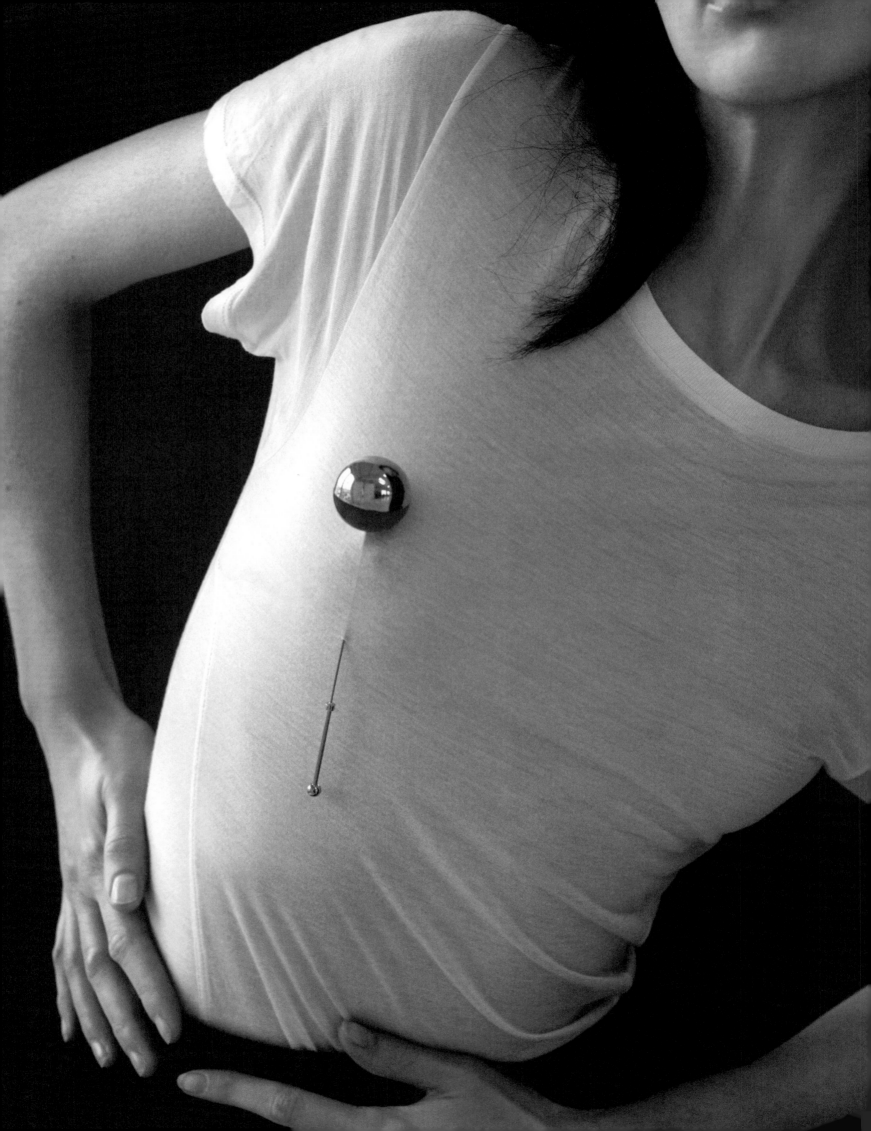

Left: White jersey body, Base Range
Black side-split skirt, Antipodium
Red and gold pin brooch, Marni

Right: Black one-shoulder top, Solace
Gold and pearl safety-pin brooch, Rosantica

Hair: Jason Crozier at SohoManagement
Make-up: Vassilis Theotokis using MAC
Model: Christina Carey at Viva Model Management London
Photography Assistant: Aaron Mavinga
Retouching: Wetouch Imagework

Paternal instinct

Words by Amei Wallach
Photography by Daniel Shea

Amei Wallach meets Rashid Johnson, the American artist who combines Joseph Beuys with Public Enemy to break down the monolithic African-American perspective

On a drippingly hot summer afternoon, on a wooded back road in the Hamptons, Rashid Johnson strides into the supersized white kitchen that anchors the expansive spaces of his country house and scoops up his three-and-a-half-year-old son Julius. Julius babbles gleefully then scrambles down. He has other things on his mind, other places to explore, preferably outdoors in the direction of the basketball hoop, leaving his father to tag behind.

Fatherhood delights and weighs on Rashid Johnson. When you are a black man in America, even a man like Johnson, who is at the forefront of a generation of young artists internationally heralded for the wide-ranging aesthetic risks they take in exploring their time and their situation, fatherhood is cause for anxiety. Fatherhood may be cause for anxiety for anyone at any time anywhere, but the stakes have always been higher if you are African-American. Julius was born on Rashid Johnson's 34th birthday, 25 September 2011. During the years of Julius's short life, scenes of the killings of unarmed young black men by white vigilantes and policemen have exposed ugly realities long unheeded and unseen. "My son had just been born when the Trayvon Martin case was happening," Johnson says, referring to the killing of an unarmed black 17-year-old by a white, self-appointed neighbourhood watchdog in February 2012. "And you even had Barack saying, 'If I had a son, this could be my son.' So I'm feeling this kind of personal space around anxiety and life change."

Johnson refers to the president of the United States as Barack in part as a mark of community and solidarity, but also because Johnson was a graduate student at the Art Institute of Chicago when Barack Obama was an Illinois State Senator. The two men first met well over a decade ago at Chicago's Museum of Contemporary Art, where Johnson was showing his work. "They'd brought Barack in to potentially try to join the junior board, which right now seems very funny," Johnson says, grinning. "Somebody had said to me, 'This guy is going to run for United States Senate.' I remember saying to him, 'Barack Obama, you're going to run for Senate? Good luck!' I said it jokingly, because I didn't think he had a chance to win."

Johnson and Obama have more in common than Chicago — where Johnson was raised and Obama came to work after law school. Like Obama, Johnson grew up in a highly educated, middle-class household; like Obama he was brainy and gifted. In his photographs, assemblages, installations, videos, paintings and sculpture the artist always makes a point of the specificity of who he is and where he comes from, as an antidote to the stereotype of the ghetto-poisoned, desperate and downtrodden African American of what he calls "the monolithic perspective". "As an artist I think my concern gets to a more personalised narrative that has to do with the way I was raised, kind of debunking the idea that every black character comes with a pre-packaged narrative that we collectively understand. We understand that slavery happened, we understand that the institution of slavery had a tremendous effect and continues to have a tremendous effect on black America today," he says. "So that is a part of the macro story, and that affects not only black Americans but the collective American consciousness. But inside of that there are the micro concerns of the individual characters. So I have to talk about my experience and my fears, my understanding of how I was affected by the greater American experience, and the good things that came from that and the more problematic things that came from that."

Johnson often exhibits a kind of intellectual distance in discussing the conceptual complexity of the work with which he probes his issues of privilege and class. His mother, Cheryl Johnson-Odim, was a professor at Northwestern University specialising in African and African-American history; his father, Jimmy Johnson — a voracious reader — owned an electronics business. But neither education nor class has shielded Rashid Johnson from the kind of anxiety that the Trayvon Martin case and the subsequent epidemic of police killings of unarmed black men reactivated around the birth of his own son. There's an unaccustomed urgency to *The Anxious Men*, the new body of work he began around that time, and to the way he talks about it.

"I was looking at Edvard Munch's *The Scream*, and I was thinking, how does an artist express the specific emotion of a time through the representation of a single face, a set of faces? If we're in a room and everybody looks terrified, it's an emotional reading we have. I wanted to create a body of work that produced an emotional reading," he says of *The Anxious Men* exhibition, which is on view at the Drawing Center in Manhattan from 2 October to 20 December. That emotion is deeply rooted in his own experience. "I remember when I was young thinking that I was illegal. Just that my physical presence was inherently illegal. It was like you're an illegal immigrant and you saw the police and you thought, 'They're not going to get me today and deport me, but they could stop me tomorrow.' I felt essentially like that all of the time — like, all of the time! Like I was illegal, so any interaction you had with the police could end in deportation and in my case that deportation would be death or prison," he says, the words pouring out with scarcely a pause for breath.

"That fear more recently has been tremendously jogged in me because of just what we've been seeing, what video and social media have opened the doors to. I think maybe there was a time when a black person would be shot by a police officer and we would all assume he must have done something that in some way made the police officer believe that they were in some way in a dangerous situation. But I think social media has made clear to all of us that these people are potentially fucking out of their minds, that they could make a decision that would end in the death of a person as a result of a systematic devaluation of that person based in part on the colour of that person's skin. That's just fucking scary!" he exclaims, his voice and every part of his body amplifying his alarm. "So I think this new work takes into account human stuff like parenting and the fact that I'd stopped boozing when I began it,

and also the relationship of my anxiety personally to a negotiation of feeling that at any given moment we could be subject to violence at the hands of validated authority figures. It's terrifying, and how do you deal with that fear? Black people should be constantly medicated! Reparations should be, like, an anti-anxiety medication like Lexapro!" he says with passionate hilarity. "That should be the start of reparations to every black American, like, here's your Valium. Because I don't know how you go through your day without *freaking out!*"

Later, over the phone, I mention Johnson's unexpected vehemence to Naomi Beckwith, director of the Museum of Contemporary Art Chicago, which mounted his mid-career travelling retrospective, *Rashid Johnson: Message to Our Folks*, in 2012. "You know what, I agree with him," she says. "We need some help. This is in the air right now – not only the police killings but also Ta-Nehisi Coates just wrote a book, *Between the World and Me*, which is a brilliant letter to his son. Right now we're at an interesting historical moment where black men are allowed to talk about themselves as emotionally vulnerable and the emotion isn't going to be anger."

While fear has played its part in the intricate web of issues Johnson weighs in his work, this new vulnerability dramatically ups the ante. "There's something very shaming about making clear you're scared. For any male there's something almost emasculating about it," he says, half-comically ending the sentence in a higher pitch. "But it's so important for us to be aware of just the amount of fear among a group that feels marginalised and subject to the power of another group." To make his point, he does what he sometimes does in his art: he holds up a kind of mirror to me, like the actual mirrors in works like *Glass Jaw*, 2011. In these wall pieces, mirrored tiles, sometimes cracked, are the background in which the viewer's distorted perception is reflected through drips of black wax and shelves of books, shea butter sculptures and objects informed with symbols of Johnson's psychic and intellectual biography. "Often times, if you can imagine, a white male or female finds themselves in what's considered to be a bad neighbourhood, and that anxiety that they potentially feel, being in that space with people who are so often desperate, potentially inspires fear in them. Now, the people living in those conditions feel that same fear, but it's permanent. So imagine that being your permanent emotional condition, as it is for people in this country who are placed in these kinds of situations with the potential outlet being incarceration, which is the most terrifying thing. I think it's considered more scary than violent death."

Johnson is attuned to nuance and incongruity. At the moment we're seated at the dining table of his own design, as he previews for me elements from *The Anxious Men* exhibition that gives form to an alarm from which there is no shelter. The table itself embodies his predilection for paradox. Its highly polished surface of solid walnut planks is long enough to comfortably accommodate a dinner party for 20, but it's branded at intervals with the cross hairs that are an integral element in his artistic

vocabulary. He appropriated the logo from the hip-hop group Public Enemy. He's simplified their silhouette of a black man caught in the cross hairs into an abstract geometry, so that this becomes a double vision from the point of view of whoever is doing the sighting, or the point of view of the sighted prey. The act of branding is a violent one, referring to slavery, but in Johnson's hands, as on the table, it's also often sardonic or decorative.

I'm sitting on one of the table's backless benches, looking through a wall of glass doors at the pool where I first spotted Johnson pacing and talking into his cellphone, like some *Saturday Night Live* send-up of the halcyon artist's life in the playground of the rich and famous. Beyond the pool are grounds so manicured, and roses so richly red that they suggest regular visits from a landscaping crew. The house is new and nearly undiminished by use. It's shingle style on the outside – sprawling with weathered shingles offset by white pillars and trim – in a nod to the regional tradition of ballooning the architectural vocabulary of colonial America into capacious holiday homes.

Inside the ceilings soar – the two storeys in the living room accommodate two stacks of full-size windows – and spaces flow into one another. The wood floors are stained dark and the walls painted white: generic decor in the Hamptons. But there are droll notes here, like the black felt with which Johnson has replaced the customary green on the pool table that, together with a major painting by the overlooked colour field painter Sam Gilliam, dominates the living room. The French doors between living room and dining room are as theoretical as the doors of a stage set. Johnson opened one and passed through to the dining room table, while I simply walked around by way of the open kitchen, where his wife, Iranian-born artist Sheree Hovsepian, was preparing aubergine, presumably from one of the abundant crop of local farm stands. As we face one another at one end of the table, Johnson is backlit by late-morning sun, and his features sometimes blur into light-struck haze. I lose the contours of his moustache and beard, but his expressions are vivid and in constant flux, his gestures at once delicate and broad, as he focuses the full force of his charisma and his attention on transmitting the contradictions in his situation, his mind and his art.

At hand he has a sample of the wallpaper with which he plans to paper the Drawing Center galleries for *The Anxious Men*, and on which he'll hang the paintings-as-drawings that, in the experimental manner of the Drawing Center, will stretch the definition of what a drawing can be. Wallpaper, with its repeated images, has been a medium in contemporary art since Andy Warhol printed his cheeky "Cow" [Pink on Yellow] wallpaper in 1966, followed by "Cow" [Yellow on Blue] in 1971. At the height of the AIDS crisis in 1989, Robert Gober contemplated his own situation as a homosexual man in America with an installation centred on his "Hanged Man/Sleeping Man" wallpaper. Its repeated drawn images depict a lynched black man and a naked sleeping white man.

Johnson himself has used wallpaper once before – in his *Smile* exhibition earlier this year at Hauser & Wirth, London. For that paper he appropriated a photograph

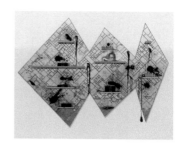

Glass Jaw, 2011.
Mirrored tile, black soap, wax, books, shea butter, vinyl, oyster shells, paint
Photo: Martin Parsekian

Crosshair Brand, 2011.
Painted steel and red oak
Photo: Genevieve Hanson

Smile, 1950 by Elliott Erwitt.
Photograph appropriated by Johnson
and tiled into wallpaper for his solo
show at Hauser & Wirth
London, January to March 2015

Green Belt, 1970

The New Black Yoga, 2011.
16mm film transferred to DVD with sound
10min 57sec duration
Photo: Genevieve Hanson

by the French-American photographer Elliott Erwitt, in which a black boy grins as he holds a gun to his head. In his far-ranging interrogations of the black dilemma, Johnson has sometimes incorporated the gallows humour nihilism of the writer Paul Beatty, who in his 1996 novel, *The White Boy Shuffle*, proposed suicide as the only plausible escape.

The image on Johnson's Drawing Center wallpaper is of his father, Jimmy, in a photograph from 1977, the year that Rashid was born. Anxious fathers make anxious men. In the photograph, father resembles his artist son, not so much in his features as in the intensity of his gaze and the need to be understood. Jimmy is seated, arms akimbo and legs open and bent so that bare feet touch. He is dressed in the loose white uniform of the Korean martial art taekwondo. "He's getting involved in self-defence, right? Like, a lot of the time what inspires us to get involved in self-defence is fear," his son comments. "So whatever fear he's dealing with he's chosen an outlet."

The artist has worked with this photograph once before in 2009, as the single image *Green Belt*. That title draws attention to the colour of the belt, only fifth in a possible ranking of 11 to the pinnacle of the black belt. In taekwondo, a green belt indicates that "the pine tree is beginning to develop and grow in strength", just one step above the camouflage belt, in which "the sapling is hidden amongst the taller pines and must now fight its way upward". Rashid Johnson's parents divorced when he was two. Most of all, like so much of Johnson's work, the photograph evokes the milieu of his boyhood in the Chicago of the 70s and 80s, when black intellectuals debated such issues as Afrocentrism, wore Afros and dashikis and soothed their skin with black wax soap and shea butter. And like Jimmy Johnson and his son Rashid, they incorporated eastern practices – Korean martial arts for the father, yoga for his son.

In the photograph that has now become wallpaper there is a bookcase behind Jimmy Johnson which is filled with a stereo and reel-to-reel tape recorder, as well as books. Often in the son's work, particularly on the shelves that he often employs in installations, the artist has incorporated copies of the books of theory, history and literature that formed him as a child and have informed his art since.

"Look at this fascinating negotiation my father has on his bookshelf, it's really interesting what he's exploring," he points out. "He's got a book called *Hidden Channels of the Mind*; he's got Malcolm X; he's got I Ching. He's trying to come to some kind of peaceful space. So it becomes about this Creole, miscegenated space he's creating." Anti-miscegenation laws criminalising sex between races were applied to unions between Aryans and Jews in Hitler's Germany, and to whites and blacks in 30 states in the US before World War II. Sixteen states still enforced those laws until 1967, when the Supreme Court declared them unconstitutional. Johnson is the only person I've ever heard use the word in this broader, metaphorical sense, with the positive intimations of internal integration.

The Jimmy Johnson photo-as-wallpaper is cropped at elbows and knees, and in repetition the image has an unsettling kaleidoscope effect, especially in conjunction, as it will be, with the blaring sound of Melvin Van Peebles's song *Love, That's America*, from his 1970 film *Watermelon Man*:

Naw this ain't America
You can't fool me.
This here's the home of the sheriff,
Not the land of the free.
In America folks don't run through the streets,
Blood streaming from where they've been beat.
And the parks are for the people
And the cops in the good old USA
Don't think they're some kind of gods, either.

Naw this ain't America
You can't fool me.

"So it's this question about what is America, how do we understand what it is, how can we become fooled by it," Johnson says, arms and smile wide.

The drawing part of the exhibition comes in the form of at least 10 portraits gouged and incised into black wax, which are mounted on the wallpaper. Shea butter and a combination of wax and African black soap are to Johnson as honey and fat were to the German post-war artist Joseph Beuys – material autobiographical expressions of alchemical transformation and transcendence.

In recent years he's been investigating and enlarging on the possibilities of his materials in ways both expressive and aesthetic. The conviction of his tangled abstract lines slashed, scored and looped in the wax/soap amalgam he calls "cosmic slop" has produced a series of stirring and beautiful paintings. After watching his striking video *The New Black Yoga* (2011) – in which black men, filmed on a beach against sky, sea and setting sun, perform slow-motion moves out of yoga interspersed with rapid, warrior-like martial leaps and thrusts – I wonder what the great 20th century art photographer Hans Namuth would record if he were to film Johnson painting, as he so famously did with Jackson Pollock in 1951. "I think it would be a hybrid," Johnson says. "It would depend on what part you came along in the process. You'd see all kinds of different approaches, some poetic, some violent, some very passive, some smaller, like a composer writing a score. And there's a lot of looking. Looking has been a big part of my project from the beginning. I think I started making art so I'd have something to look at."

Instead of flooring or mirrored tile – his alternative to canvas in past works – for *The Anxious Men* exhibition Johnson has splashed his black wax portraits on bright white bathroom tile. These are portraits in only the most abstract and elemental sense, the way the French artist Jean Dubuffet's naif heads in sand, tar and straw are portraits, or the African-American sculptor Melvin Edwards's masks welded from locks, chains and manacles.

In Johnson's portraits for the Drawing Center it looks as if the melted soap and black wax have been flung onto

the white tiles, like tattered rags sweating grime. Cat's cradles of coiled lines excavated to the white beneath describe the bulbous eyes. Mouths are frantic white scratches, blotted, scraped or distended over chicken-thin necks. "The anxiety and the technique produces almost — I want to call it a desperation to start to unfold a face in the short period of time, maybe five minutes, that you're given with the soap before it hardens," Johnson says. I mention that there's something harrowing about these black humanoid geometries against the white bathroom tile. "The tile is supposed to be easy to clean," Johnson says. "Like we can get rid of these splattered heads because you've done it on something we've made easy to clean." The effect is exacerbated when he holds up the wallpaper of his father behind one of his flayed heads. The white of his father's martial costume is not nearly so white as the bathroom tile, and the dialogue between the two is chilling. "It is," Johnson agrees. "And when you hear the music behind it, it's just fucking nuts. But it's exactly where I feel I am." When I describe the work to the MCA's Beckwith, she makes a connection to the artist Glenn Ligon's appropriation of a line from the Harlem Renaissance writer Zora Neale Hurston: "I feel most colored when I am thrown against a sharp white background."

As always with Johnson, there's more than one side to the story, though. These abstract heads also have the presence of Byzantine icons. The wallpaper functions as a kind of iconostasis on which icons are hung. Because, for Johnson, white tile isn't only an emblem of the black lives that don't seem to matter, it's also as sacred to him as the gold halos of the saints to a worshipper in a Russian Orthodox church. Throughout his life, in moments of stress and transition, anxiety has driven him to seek succour, not only in psychiatry but in regenerative experiences that eventually find their way into his work. When he was in graduate school at the Art Institute of Chicago around 2003 he was going through a divorce, and a friend suggested he try for tranquillity at the Division Street Russian and Turkish Baths, where you could sit all day for $20 and read while you sweated. Sometimes Johnson had to borrow the $20, but he was hooked.

"It was a fascinating place. Jesse Jackson was there and all the reverends; the Mexican business community would be there, and communists. It became like this melting pot of these amazing thinkers, all naked, all in this room, and these overlapping conversations, because these guys all knew each other. They'd been going there for 30 years," Johnson recalls, outlined in light at the table in his Hamptons dining room. "And I started going there. I'd Xerox whatever I was reading, like Derrida's *The Gift of Death*, or Sartre, all this incredibly dense critical theory or philosophy. And I'd look up at these dirtyish white tiles, and when you're reading and you look up at white space it's almost as if the words are projected onto the space, and you wait until it fades, this blankness. And it was this really comforting thing to look at, this very safe thing for me."

He realised that growing up in a family that wasn't in the least religious he'd never had that kind of space consecrated to self-exploration. "I understand how he'd find a sacred space in a steam room," says Beckwith. "Part of anxiety and depression is feeling alone, and one safe space for the black community was the church. But he was separated from that. In the 70s and 80s many people left the church." They turned to eastern philosophies. Except for brief experiments with bathroom tiles, Johnson has only used his steam-room experiences once — when he staged a reimagination of *Dutchman* by LeRoi Jones (better known as Amiri Baraka) in the Russian & Turkish Baths on the Lower East Side of Manhattan in 2013. But for the Drawing Center works the tiles seemed right, intimating not only the anxiety of fatherhood and the fear endemic to a black father in America but also, like a Byzantine icon, offering the possibility of transcendence in a sacred space — undercut, of course by the audio shriek of *Love, That's America*.

The Anxious Men exhibition owes much of its emotional weight to the fact that it is in every sense a family project. Johnson's father Jimmy is present in the wallpaper, his son Julius in the impulse for the work, and his mother Cheryl Johnson-Odim in the inclusion of her poetry and stories in the exhibition catalogue.

The themes of the stories are suicide and rape. In *The Road to Hell*, a young girl seeks her own peaceful space in a dark cellar, amidst "floating microscopic particles of cement, coal dust, the scent of mice droppings", where she hides from the assaults of her stepfather and dreams of murdering him. The poems consider alternatives to such dilemmas as "walking tightropes pulled taut above seas of enemies". An essay/story about "Abuela Ruth", pays tribute to a role model who taught the writer to "skip among the landmines of life" instead of settling for compromise.

Johnson credits his mother for what I've always considered his uncommon self-possession in overcoming early fame at the age of 23. In 2001 he became the youngest artist included in the Studio Museum in Harlem's now legendary exhibition *Freestyle*, introducing what came controversially to be called the post-black generation. Johnson was presented in that exhibition as a photographer and singled out for the tragic poetry of his close-up silver gelatin portraits of individual homeless black men.

"My mother was an historian, so the emphasis in my home was often about legacy and the larger scope of history," he explains. Instead of being tempted, as far too many young artists would be, to seize the Freestyle moment "to produce a career, for me it was more about developing a language and a way of working that I thought I could do for the rest of my life. It's the collective project that I have the most investment in," he declares. In any case, by the time that exhibition opened he was already deep into a new body of work, such as *The Unwearable Dashiki*, which he created in 2001. He started to play with symbolism and abstraction, recalling feasts from his childhood by exposing negative photosensitive images of chicken bones, lentils and black-eyed peas in the early stages of what has become a catholic embrace of methods and message.

It's an endlessly faceted message. Johnson is all too aware of the ways in which meanings change while situations stay the same. His grandparents, as Julie Rodrigues Widholm, curator of his MCA retrospective, points out, were once referred to as negros, his parents as blacks. His little sister was born into an age of African-American as the accepted term. He himself uses black and African-American interchangeably, which gives me permission to do likewise. The dreadlocks hairstyle he has been wearing since his teenage years, when it signified an anti-establishment stance, has morphed in meaning and popularity until now when, he notes, "you see a lot of football players with it. I would like to cut it off, but I think I'm starting to go bald. Now it's just an ageing man trying to figure out what to do with his body," says the artist, who is 38.

He sometimes uses his body in photographs as he seeks to understand and expand — whether with humour, nihilism or the new emotionality — what it is to be a black man in America. "I think the most honest thing I could talk about with clarity is my maleness and my blackness. It's the thing I know best," he says, as we rise from the table. "There's this trope that's preached about write what you know. I feel like I'm attempting virtue by being as honest and clear as I can."

Integral to that honesty as a black man is a clarity about his privilege and his education. "If we identify that we're completely cognisant that those privileges exist and how those privileges affect other people, and could potentially be handicapping to other people, that is a starting point," he says. "I'm not exactly sure what the next step is, and I would never suggest that I would be in a position to cure society's ills, but cognisance seems to me like a *great* place to start." And that is why curator Widholm is convinced that Johnson "has found a way through his material vocabulary to make work that speaks to concerns that are at once very personal and universal. It's about being who you are, and about the freedom to be who you are."

Behind the scenes in Rashid Johnson's Brooklyn studio

The colour of shape

Photography by Rory van Millingen
Styling by Victoria Sekrier

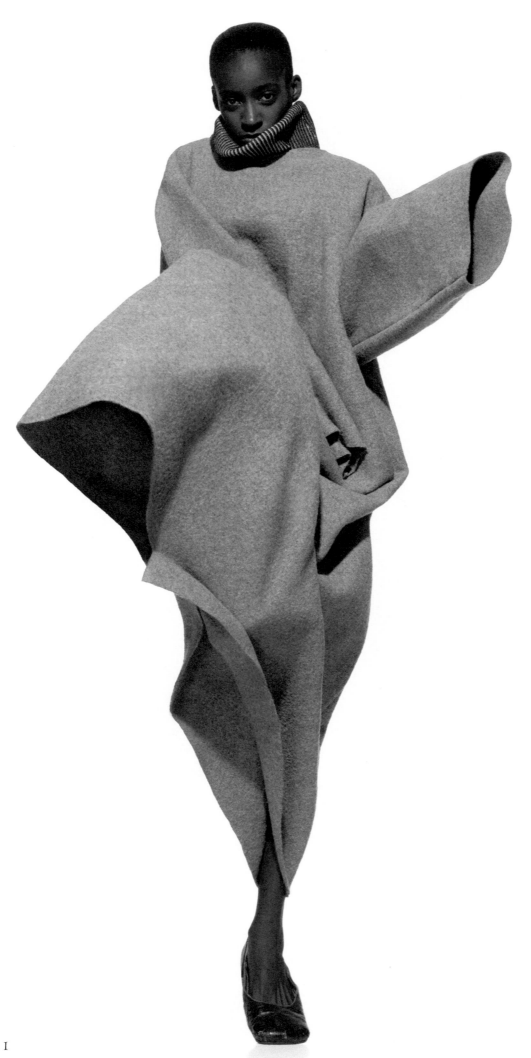

Casting Director: Paul Isaac
Model: Viviane Oliveira at MC2
Hair: Daniel Martin at D+V Management
Make-up: Nobuko Maekawa using MAC
Photography Assistant: Jack Symes
Stylist Assistant: Surgil Khan

page 26
Jumper, Finery
Top, Barbara Casasola
Culottes, Céline
Gloves, stylist's own
Shoes (worn throughout), courtesy of National Theatre Archive

page 27
Shirt, Yohji Yamamoto
Dress, Joseph
Tights, Wolford

page 28
Cape, Loewe
Trousers, Yohji Yamamoto
Tights, Wolford

page 29
Dress, Marques' Almeida
Dress (underneath), Proenza Schouler
Trousers, Rosetta Getty
Gloves, stylist's own

page 30
Top, Stella McCartney
Padded vest, Richard Malone
Skirt, Issey Miyake
Gloves, stylist's own

page 31
Sweater (worn as neck piece), Adam Selman
Robe, courtesy of National Theatre Archive

page 32
Knitted dress, Marques' Almeida
Trousers, Marni
Skirt, Yohji Yamamoto archive courtesy of Storm in a Teacup
Scarf, Issey Miyake

page 33
Roll-neck sweater dress, Bernhard Willhelm
Sweater dress, Stella McCartney
Tights, Wolford

page 34
Coat courtesy of National Theatre Archive
Trousers, A.W.A.K.E.
Tights, Wolford

page 35
Jumper, Finery
Dress, Stella McCartney
Trousers, Barbara Casasola
Scarf, Issey Miyake
Gloves, stylist's own

The happiness industry

Interview by Justin Quirk
Illustrations by Rune Fisker

Your feelings are now a valuable
commodity. *Supplement* meets
the man who knows why

Will Davies is senior lecturer in politics at Goldsmiths, University of London, and co-director of the political economy research centre at the university. His new book, *The Happiness Industry*, looks at what a Buddhist monk was doing at the 2014 World Economic Forum at Davos lecturing world leaders on mindfulness, why so many successful corporations have a "chief happiness officer", and why potential employers want to know the chemical composition of your brain. In the past decade, governments and corporations have become increasingly interested in measuring the way people feel. As a result, he argues, our emotions have become a new resource to be bought and sold.

Justin Quirk: *How did the idea take shape?*

Will Davies: It began as I was finishing my PhD around 2008-2009, and the financial crisis exploded. As a sociologist I was interested in how economics is used to make policy decisions and as a way to analyse the world, and how economics shapes the way we think. I was looking at the financial crisis and thinking, 'This is it. This is the big one; this is the end of a whole kind of political economic paradigm.'

JQ: *And it probably came much closer to that than people realise…*

WD: It probably did, yeah. People like [BBC economics editor] Robert Peston said that at the time he thought he was watching the equivalent of 1989 for state socialism, that this was going to be the end, and that something else was going to come along very, very dramatically. But it didn't happen and I became interested in how economists had managed to rescue their paradigm. One of the ways the economics profession was explaining and interpreting what had happened – at the same time sustaining their own view of the world – was to locate the source of problems in the mind or body. Neuro-economists were saying that our brains release the wrong kind of neurochemical and therefore people take bad decisions in financial markets. Some of this is almost entertainingly bullshit.

JQ: *Stuff like 'Financial traders releasing too much testosterone at the wrong times'?*

WD: Yeah, or they're taking too much cocaine. Behavioural economics had a massive surge around this time because what it says, broadly, is that markets are absolutely fine, but every now and again people miscalculate their decisions or what's in our interest. And that's why people become obese or they buy things that they don't really want. There was this massive grab for quite simplistic psychological arguments, partly as a way to rescue economics. I became interested in economic psychology because it seemed to be playing an important role in sustaining what you might call neoliberalism. I started reading around how economists had tried to understand the mind, and what happens when economics becomes interested in questions about happiness or behaviour or emotions. I started to trace these historically and realised that economists had actually become interested in this in the late 19th century. In a way it's a book about capitalism and efforts to try and bring the mind or body into regimes of management and profit maximisation. Happiness is an instrument towards that end.

JQ: *So, essentially, are we saying that you have two choices when a financial system crashes: either there's something inherently wrong with the system, or we can blame it on the people and the minds working within it? Did they essentially go with the latter because the former is just too frightening to consider?*

WD: I think this is a theme that runs through a lot of the happiness industry: these experts look at the relationship between economic circumstances and the mind and how the two relate to each other. As you say, when things start to go wrong the question is, do you focus your critique on the institutions and the circumstances, or do you focus your critique on the mind, behaviour, feelings and so on? It's not just in the financial crisis; in a wide range of other situations there is a tendency to look at the latter – which in a way absolves the circumstances and these institutions from blame or from proper inspection.

JQ: *Can you give us a more concrete example?*

WD: In Britain, look at the way Workfare is employing psychological theories to try and get people back to work. You have people who are out of work and suffer from chronic psychosomatic health problems – they might be depressed, eating very badly, have lifestyles that basically mean that they're not really able to work – but a lot of the happiness-economics techniques are deployed in an effort to reactivate those people. It's telling them, 'Come on, be more positive, think better, think different, get out of bed earlier.' It's a benefit-sanctions regime that is constantly 'at' people.

But all of that rests on the assumption that our model of capitalism is basically the right one, and that people have to adapt or be retrained or reconfigured or reprogrammed in order to be more entrepreneurial or more competitive or more optimistic about their situation. What that does is to lose what could be a political energy that might say, 'Well actually, no, we've had enough of this; this system is no longer working.'

JQ: *I found the idea that chronic, low-level illness may be a kind of passive rebellion against the workplace was really interesting. Do you think there's something in that?*

WD: Health, in physical and mental varieties, has become a major concern for HR and for management. And that has both an elite manifestation, where very high-value workers are treated almost like racehorses – you have to keep walking, you have to have a Fitbit, you have to have a really good free high-nutritional-value lunch laid on like in the Google campus – and a bottom end, where you've got people who are falling in and out of work with psychosomatic problems. This, in a country like Britain with a socialised health system, is a problem for the state because those people [at the bottom] end up going to the doctor. And in between you get a lot of white-collar work where people get stressed or they have chronic mental-health problems – such as depression or anxiety – which they don't talk to their managers about because they don't know how, and nor does the manager. In one way or another, chronic questions of health have become entangled in work and questions of productivity.

JQ: *And this is something that managers are aware of?*

WD: Managers are terrified of it because they don't know what to do about it. But ultimately it has to be understood in a more political sense… Now when their health breaks down, people don't tend to come out and say 'I refuse', because the channels for that kind of voice in the workplace have deteriorated since the 1970s, so people go into some kind of collapse.

JQ: *Although if you're being more sceptical, is there not also an argument that we live in a society that is now more predicated on individualism and the self, and being in touch with your feelings, so people just express stuff in a way they wouldn't have done 20 years ago?*

WD: That may be true, but I think… Maybe you could say there's a fundamental conflict in our society where, on the one hand everyone wants to be emotionally well and healthy, and therefore when they feel under pressure they start to speak in those terms, but on the other hand everyone wants to be a very high-performance, highly competitive individual, which actually is not a recipe for emotional well-being. So that's the conflict. I think people like Richard Layard, the happiness guru, are well aware that in some ways the culture of high-competition, high-performance neoliberal capitalism is very bad for happiness. The problem is that as an economist, someone like Layard doesn't go and question the broader structures that generate it.

JQ: *There's that Matthew Collings line where he talks about going into the National Gallery and 'stepping off the capitalist death march' by looking at some paintings for a bit.*

WD: We all have things like that, but some of it becomes a bit mandated. The most extreme story I heard recently was at a talk I did in Philadelphia. There was a guy in the audience who told me that he worked in a casino and once a week they got together with their boss and everyone had to dance to Pharrell Williams's *Happy* – they had to. The idea of enforced dancing always has a very, very dark edge to it, I think.

JQ: *Could you pinpoint a time where happiness in its broadest sense went from being this desirable goal to something that was seen as productive and useful and something you had to strive for? Is it as simple as, 'In 1979 everything changed'?*

WD: Psychologists have been consulted by managers since the early 20th century. What's called industrial psychology begins after World War I, where psychologists start to study workplaces to try and calculate how people can work harder. Then by the late 1920s people like Elton Mayo – who's often seen as the founder of HR – was arguing that you've got to start taking the emotional well-being of your employees seriously; that's the way to get them to work harder.

There's a chapter in the book about the period between 1960 and 1980, when various things emerge. You get the discovery of antidepressants in the late 1950s, and a complete change in the way in which depression is viewed. Where depression for Freud was a kind of neurotic relationship with oneself and one's past and something that had to be disentangled… depression starts to manifest itself in a different way over the course of the 60s and 70s as something that comes to look more and more medical, and I suppose that's partly because of the discovery of antidepressants.

JQ: *And is this around the same time as the Diagnostic Statistical Manual?*

WD: Yeah, the *DSM-III* was published in 1980 and is a key moment in psychiatry, and really reinforces this very medical, very technical view of mental health. And I think that what comes out of that is the idea that emotions – and positive emotions in particular – need to be managed and constantly propped up and optimised… By the 90s people were talking about the brain and there was a sort of neuroculture of thinking about emotions as these quasi-physical things – a bit like physical fitness – that need to be tended and optimised.

JQ: *Is there any parallel at all with the decline of religion? Because there are things I was thinking about that kept popping up when I read the book, where a lot of it almost sounded like a secular version of what organised religion used to do – this idea that you're created sick and then commanded to be good. There seemed like an element of 'No one's happy and no one's working hard enough but you've got to strive for it anyway.'*

WD: Various people have written about the problem with 60s culture and thereafter, that it says you've got to be authentic to yourself; you've got to be utterly fulfilled and you've got to be hedonistic; you've got to live life to the full and so on – and it makes happiness harder because you then start to feel like a failure when you're not doing those things the whole time. And I think that's a very strong feeling that people, particularly young people, have today. Facebook makes it worse because everyone puts up happy photos of themselves, and then other people feel bad and they have to put up a happy photo.

JQ: *Where do you see all this going? Do you see all the stuff – nudge units etc – as a fad that's going to be fairly short-lived and there'll be something else in three years' time?*

WD: I think Silicon Valley – and a lot of it's around MIT and Cambridge – is pretty fixated on this being the future. I think the technological investments in making emotions and well-being measurable are huge. That has a certain sort of inevitability – once enough capital goes into something being the future, then it is a self-fulfilling prophecy. People are saying that at the moment the Apple Watch only collects data about your body but soon it'll be about your emotions, whatever that means. Mark Zuckerberg has said – I think in a fascinating, although utopian, way – that the end goal of Facebook is telepathy. Instead of us having to communicate using words, we will just be able to have the identical experience that someone else is having somewhere else. Equally, things like smart cities are all about 'Could we start to detect the emotions of crowds, the feelings of crowds and so on in order to anticipate problems as they arise?' There's a lot of commitment to this stuff.

JQ: *But a lot of that assumes, as a lot of economic models do, that people are rational.*

WD: Not necessarily rational.

JQ: *Or at least honest about their feelings, that what they're writing on Twitter is actually what they think or feel.*

WD: It certainly assumes a more kind of behaviourist assumption that people can be monitored in that way, that the data that people generate through their bodies, their tweets, their faces, is a decent predictor of what's going to happen – that's the core behaviourist assumption. I think that behaviourist exuberance has had waves in the past, and they've tended to run out of steam

eventually… I think that people making very strong claims that they can understand what other people are feeling purely through data will start to take on a slightly ridiculous air. It's difficult to say exactly how that will come about. There's a neuromarketer called Martin Lindstrom who I quote in the book. His slogan, on which he's basically built his career, is 'People lie, but brains don't': meaning that you can, if you observe people in the right way, find out what's really going on. No one in neuroscience would ever actually say that.

JQ: *But it's a great line.*

WD: It's a great line, but they would throw up their hands in horror. Data analysts working inside Facebook or Google would probably tell you the things that we can really know about people are pretty messy. But then these urban myths start to emerge about how Google can tell you when your wife's pregnant before you or she knows. Of course they have something in them, but I think the heavy rationalism side of it will eventually run out of steam because it's palpably nonsense, the idea that we are now on the right path, and we're just going to get closer and closer to the truth of humanity.

JQ: *Are you going to turn from poacher to gamekeeper at some point? Presumably you now have a stack of knowledge that you could retool in a certain way and wander into the Google campus.*

WD: I actually got invited to give a TEDx talk at the London Google office, but it was on the topic of fun. I thought, either they hadn't actually read my book or I'd been invited to come along and just go 'Yeah, fun's shit', and I couldn't really be bothered to do either, so I didn't accept it.

JQ: *Would it have made you happy, though? That's the thing.*

WD: I don't know. It would've been an interesting experience. I thought of going and doing what in ethno-methodology is called a breaching experiment, where you just turn up and – almost like a Situationist prank – go in and give such an absurd talk about how fun could add 100 per cent of productivity, and see if anybody actually noticed. It would be quite interesting to see if they did.

JQ: *I imagine everyone would just go along with it.*

WD: Yeah, if it was on video then it could be a great viral hit. But I'm not sure I'd really have the guts to do it. *potlatch.typepad.com*

The Happiness Industry is out now, published by Verso

Rising high

Interview by Cath Clarke
Photography by Mark Peckmezian / Styling by Ellie Grace Cumming

How has 24-year-old actress Stacy Martin managed to model
for Miu Miu and make eight films in the last three years?
"Wow, I was really, really lucky," she says

Stacy Martin is looking forward to the next few months, when she can finally talk about acting without her porn double or prosthetic vagina casually dropping into conversation. Right now, Stacy admits, she is "that girl from *Nymphomaniac*" – famous for playing a young sex addict in Lars von Trier's eccentric provocation on female desire. As big splashes go, they don't come splashier. The 24-year-old has skipped the struggling years – bit parts on TV, acting in rubbish plays watched by four people in a freezing cold theatre.

We meet during a week-long gap in her busy schedule – one of the few breaks she's had all year. And what a year. She has made seven films since *Nymphomaniac*, including *High-Rise*, British director Ben Wheatley's forthcoming adaptation of JG Ballard's 1975 dystopian tower-block thriller, as well as appearing in two Miu Miu campaigns and becoming the face of its first fragrance. You can see why Miuccia Prada picked her as her muse for Miu Miu – the young and free, naïve little sister to Prada. In person, Stacy is warm and funny, calmly navigating us at eight in the morning to the nearest coffee shop with her iPhone – Miu Miu bag hooked on her arm. The coffee shop, it turns out, closed down six weeks ago, so we give up and head back to the studio, where she drinks black coffee: "I can barely speak without coffee this early."

Her accent is boarding-school cut-glass, despite the fact that she didn't live in the UK until her late teens. Half-French, half-English, Stacy was born in France. Her family moved to Tokyo when she was seven, before returning to Paris. She escaped to London aged 18 to take a degree in media and cultural studies. "Sorry if I forget the words," she says with a grin as we start. "I know them in french, and just try to say them with an English accent."

Left: Navy corduroy jacket, Chloé
Striped silk shirt, Modes & More

Cath Clarke: *So much has happened to you over the past 18 months or so. Have you caught up?*

Stacy Martin: Not really. It's been crazy and really exciting. All the films I've made are coming out now, so it's quite a nice moment – it becomes real.

CC: *Actresses in their twenties often talk about struggling to find decent roles. You've somehow managed to find seven of them. How?*

SM: I always speak to the director, because you can read an amazing script, then talk to the director and realise that what they want to do with this piece of writing is not what you had imagined. You have to be really careful.

CC: *Is it hard to turn down work when you're so near the beginning of your career?*

SM: Yes, I hate it. But you have to be really honest about what you want to do. If you start doing things that you don't connect to, ultimately that's going to affect the rest. So you have to be really strict with yourself. The weird thing about me is that I started with Lars, so I feel like it gave me a head start.

CC: *Was that an odd moment, when Nymphomaniac came out, to go from complete unknown to everyone talking about you?*

SM: It was strange, because we shot the film and it came out about a year later. So for a whole year there was all the gossip. Even if people hadn't seen it, they already had an opinion. I knew the film would have a profile, I just didn't expect it to suddenly become: 'Oh, this is Stacy Martin'.

CC: *Which of the films you've made since Nymphomaniac are you most looking forward to unleashing on the world?*

SM: I've just got back from Venice where I just saw *The Childhood of a Leader*.

CC: *This is about the early years of a future fascist leader, set during World War I?*

SM: Yes. So it's half-fiction, half-based on historical fact. It's quite a dark film; the storyline doesn't matter so much as the atmosphere. The director Brady Corbet worked so hard, so to watch him present his film was incredibly emotional. Everyone got a bit teary. We were all just crying. So I'm really excited to see that. I play Aida, the French tutor who teaches the young boy.

CC: *Do you find yourself being drawn towards darker films? Is that where you instinctively go?*

SM: Maybe you're right. But also, I just haven't read that much comedy that I really connect to. As a woman it's very difficult to find comedy in which you're not the dumb girlfriend or boring girl next door.

CC: *You worked as a model before you acted, while you were at university. Did you enjoy it?*

SM: No. Not because it was a horrible job. It's just not what I wanted to do. I wasn't sure what I wanted to do at that stage, so in that sense it was great, rather than working in pubs or restaurants. Some of my friends were working three jobs and studying at the same time. Modelling gave me a lot of freedom. I could pay my own rent as soon as I stepped out of my parents' home. People still struggle at 30. I kind of look back at it and think: wow, I was really, really lucky, but I'm glad I got out of it.

CC: *You were still taking acting classes when you got the part of Joe in Nymphomaniac. How nerve-wracking was that?*

SM: I treated the casting as a continuation of being in class. I couldn't even imagine getting the part. I never thought that Lars would cast someone completely unknown. He can work with whoever he wants. I didn't even have an agent at that time. But I think I was ready to work, mentally: yes, I'm going to do my best and hopefully it'll work out. I was really motivated to do it.

CC: *Do you suffer from nerves?*

SM: Yes, all the time. I think all actors do, because you do something that means so much to you. I'm really nervy.

CC: *Were you anxious about working with Lars von Trier? He's known for difficult relationships with actresses.*

SM: No, weirdly. I read this script – and it was one of the first scripts I'd read. It was about 300 pages long and it was a piece of literature in its own right. I fell in love with it. And I love Lars's work. I think he deals with issues and problems and gender in a way that no other director does. All the gossip

Left: Black velvet cape, Simone Rocha
Black distressed knit jumper, Corbier Agostini
White net top, Phoebe English

Right: Black brushed cotton roll-neck dress, Vetements
Drop crystal earrings (held in hand), Vetements
Tights, Falke
All rings, Stacy's own

about his reputation kind of became secondary. What mattered was how we got on. And we did get along, thank God. It's not the kind of film where you can go in a conflict with the director.

CC: *You had an interesting childhood. You were born in France then lived in Japan. What took your family there?*

SM: My dad always always dreamed of living in Japan. He went to Tokyo when he was younger and just fell in love with it. So he opened his own hair salon there and we lived there for about six or seven years.

CC: *How did you feel moving back to Paris as a teenager?*

SM: It was very strange. I kept saying to my mum, 'All the cars have scratches and there's dog crap on the ground. Everyone's depressed on the Metro and they're not organised.'

CC: *Do you think your upbringing helps you in your work as an actor? Not having a sense of belonging?*

SM: I don't know. People always ask me, 'What's French in you and what's

English in you?' I have no idea. I say no a lot, which is very Parisian. But I'm always saying sorry, which is English. But I don't have the mecca of home. Home doesn't have sanctity for me. My home is where I am at that moment. But you do feel quite unrooted sometimes as an actor, travelling all the time. You just don't really know what you're doing.

CC: *What are your earliest childhood memories?*

SM: Eating ice cream. A lot of my memories are based around food. My dad has an extremely big family and they organise huge dinners. That's what I remember, the sound of everyone; they're very loud, bon vivants.

CC: *What were you into as a kid? Were you the little girl putting on plays in the back garden?*

SM: No, not at all. But when I was about eight I remember a lady knocking at the door, a pollster, and she asked me what I wanted to do. Out of nowhere I said, 'Oh, I want to be an actress.' But then I wanted to be a horse-riding teacher, I wanted to be an astronaut, a ballet dancer.

Left & Right: Black vinyl crocodile coat, Miu Miu

CC: *You've shot two Miu Miu campaigns and you're the face of the fragrance. What do you admire about Miuccia Prada?*

SM: Her tenacity. She's an incredible woman. She always challenges herself. There's this sense of never doing the same thing. She's always pushing forward and branching out. So her work doesn't just stay within fashion, it reaches out to other spheres of culture. With the Miu Miu Tales she helps female directors make short films. And she's just opened the Fondazione Prada. She has this real energy to help women.

CC: *What's your approach to style?*

SM: I don't really have one. Quite simple, quite minimal, fuss-free I guess. With Miu Miu and going to events, your style does change. I understand it a bit more than before.

CC: *Do you have any rules when it comes to being styled for events? Is there anything you try to avoid?*

SM: I thought I had rules. But the funny thing about Miu Miu and Prada is that they'll bring outfits out and I think: I am never going to put that on. That is just insane. And I just try it on and actually it feels really comfortable. It doesn't feel like I'm overly dressed or I'm not me. But my aim is to make sure I can sit down comfortably, go to the toilet and not stray too far from who I am.

CC: *Can you bear to watch yourself on screen?*

SM: No. I try to. I think it's important. It's just very difficult to get past the self-criticism. It's very easy to watch myself and think, 'Look at my eye twitching'. No one else can see it. But I'm remembering, associating it with how nervous I was or how bad I thought it went. I am working on it though. I try to watch the takes. Even then, I immediately start panicking, which means I get self-conscious during the take. So it's a work in progress.

CC: *You seem very focused on the kind of career that you want to have, working with interesting art-house directors. After the Nymphomaniac films did you have lots of offers from Hollywood?*

SM: No. I don't think the studios really understood them. And it's not like I turn down anything. I'm really open to working in any field, as long as there is something about it that interests me. That's the most important thing. I'm still learning how to choose the right director. I don't have a plan or have a goal to achieve. I just want to collaborate with directors and actors that are on the same page. Ultimately I want to do things that I can look back on and say, 'I was in this film and I'm pretty proud of that.' If everything stops I can say, 'Well I've worked with Lars von Trier. I've worked with Ben Wheatley.'

CC: *Are there any actors you look at and think: I'd quite like a career that looks a bit like that?*

SM: Yes, a lot of them. Rooney Mara is clever. She does big studio films and then really great independent films. But it's difficult because you look at these actors who've worked really hard to get to where they are, but ultimately it's their career because it's them. What makes you you and what makes me me is different. I try not to think about it too much. I'll never be able to do what Rooney Mara does because there's not going to be the same films. We're different and we have different sensibilities and opinions and tastes. I try and just make my own career and we'll see.

CC: *What are you reading right now?*

SM: I just finished the Lena Dunham book *Not That Kind of Girl*. I was reading lots of Gertrude Stein and Susan Sontag and realised I actually hadn't really read much contemporary writing.

High-Rise is due to be released in early 2016

High-rise
Film market image
Designed by Jay Shaw

Left: Navy ribbed cotton jumper, Marques' Almeida
Patterned silk trousers, Vivienne Westwood

Set Design: Theo Palitowicz at Magnet
Make-up: Lotten Holmqvist at Julian Watson Agency using MAC
Hair: Naoki Komiya at Julian Watson Agency
Photography Assistants: Ian Bird and Joe Wilson
Stylist Assistant: Jordan Duddy
Make-up Assistant: Emma Broom
Hair Assistant: Kumiko Tsumagari
Set Design Assistant: Bon Walsh
Production: Webber Represents

Insta

Photography by Paul Maffi

Model: Tilda Lindstam at IMG
Hair: Bok-Hee at Streeters
Make-up: Georgi Sandev at Streeters
Production: Amanda Lokey
Clothing: Tilda's own

CHILDREN
OF THE COAL

Photography by Albert Watson
Styling by Paul Sinclaire

Hair: Rudy Martins for L'Atelier
Make-up: Alice Lane at The Wall Group and Mariko Hirano
Casting: Barbara Pfister
Producer: Walker Hinerman

Models:
Lucas and Stanson at Ford
Matthieu, Ted and Matt at DNA
Anders at Request
Harvey at New York Models
Lou and Marland at New York Models

page 67
Brocade blouse, Dries Van Noten
Lady slipper from ZeZe Flowers, NYC

page 68
Cotton sweatshirt, Olderbrother
Trousers, Dries Van Noten
Sterling silver money clip, Tiffany & Co

page 70
Fur-collared wool coat, Dries Van Noten

page 71
Left: Cotton sweatshirt, Olderbrother
Trousers, Dries Van Noten
Sterling silver money clip, Tiffany & Co
Right: Wool trousers, Dries Van Noten

page 73
Left: Wool coat, Dries Van Noten
Right: Wool trousers, Dries Van Noten
59Fifty baseball cap, New Era, from Hat Club NYC

page 74
Vintage wool blazer, Dries Van Noten
Diamond Slice necklace, Monique Pean
Trousers, Dries Van Noten

page 75
Vintage cotton shirt, Dries Van Noten
Grosgrain ribbon, Mokuba
Braces, American Apparel

page 76
Fur-collared wool coat, Dries Van Noten

page 77
Left: Silk military style shirt, Dries Van Noten
Right: Silk brocade jacket, Dries Van Noten
Trousers, Dries Van Noten
59Fifty baseball cap, New Era, from Hat Club NYC

page 78
Cotton sweatshirt, Olderbrother
Trousers, Dries Van Noten
Sterling silver money clip, Tiffany & Co

page 79
Matte black riding hat, Bern Unlimited
Metallic brocade vest, sequined bomber vest, both Dries Van Noten
Dinosaur bone and diamond earring, Monique Pean

page 81
Silk and cotton shirt, Dries Van Noten
Wool trousers, Dries Van Noten

After Ghost Ranch

Photography by Rory Payne
Styling by Verity Parker

Previous: Shirt and skirt, both Y's by Yohji Yamamoto / Left: Shirt, Y's by Yohji Yamamoto. Skirt, Joseph / Right: Dress, Rosetta Getty

Left: Dungarees, APC / Right: Dress, Lemaire. Jacket, Raquel Allegra. Hat, The Carrier Company

Left: Shirt, Debris London. Trousers, Equipment / Right: Shirt (tied around waist), APC. Skirt, Y's by Yohji Yamamoto

Previous left: Artist smock, Debris London. Trousers, Margaret Howell / Right: Shirt and trousers, MiH. Apron, Debris London
This spread left: Shirt, Paul Smith. Apron, Debris London / Right: Dress, Rochas

Model: Valerija Kelava at Tess Management / Hair: Nao Kawakami at Saint Luke Artists / Make-up: Jenny Coombs at Streeters
Photography Assistant: Lewis Hayward / Digital Operator: Mark Simpson / Stylist Assistant: Dee Moran / Casting: Sophie Castley for LOCK / Location: North6

Rollin' swollen

Words by Justin Quirk
Photography by Jeff Boudreau / Styling by Andrew Davis

**How did Britain become a country where fitness,
muscles and gym culture are the norm among
young men — and what is it doing to them?**

It's almost midnight when I leave the train station on the edge of Zone 6 in London. It's a Thursday and, bar a few commuters and post-work drinkers straggling back on the last train of the evening and a couple of takeaways that are closing up, the town centre is dead.

With one notable exception. An entire floor of a vast, modernist office block overlooking the railway tracks — an enormous white elephant that has never been fully occupied since it first opened in the 1960s — has recently become a glass-sided, 24-hour gym. An idea that within recent memory would have seemed like something from a satirical guide to yuppie life in Singapore is now an unremarkable reality, even in the most humdrum suburbs. As the clock strikes midnight, lines of people march endlessly on cross-trainers and lift weights, burn fat and build muscle. This is Britain in 2015 — where gym culture has grown and swollen from being a slightly uncouth niche pursuit to the dominant leisure activity, a huge industry and an influence on everything from fashion to physical form. How did we get here? And is it good for us?

More than 7.5 million British adults now belong to a gym or leisure centre, an all-time high number (the first chain gym only opened in 1993, making this growth genuinely impressive). The economic downturn that followed 2008 did little to dampen the British public's enthusiasm for paying to work out, although budget outfits like The Gym Group did emerge in response to limited finances and the industry is now estimated to be a £4.3 billion concern.

How the gyms now view themselves is telling: Fitness First recently came back from the brink of financial collapse, and its rebranding was overseen not by anyone with a background in sport, but by Andy Cosslett, a former executive of InterContinental Hotels, and was firmly rooted in turning the company into a lifestyle provider, rather than just a place to get fit. Behavioural psychologists were consulted, talking in terms of "personal growth", "autonomy" and "a sense of belonging". Staff were retrained in the manner of hotel personnel. "Andy Cosslett's view is that we are a hospitality business," said Mark Hutcheons, director of communications for the group. "People choose to come here. We needed to ask them 'What do you want?'"

Twenty years ago, when I was first a student, the only people who used the gym were sports-science students and members of the rugby team — dull, lumpy types who didn't much like music and wore sports kit into bars before standing around massive, space-blocking holdalls the way that women used to crowd around piles of handbags. If you'd asked them what they wanted, the answer would probably just have been "more squat racks", not something about community, development and iPad-based instructional videos. However, the bastard sons and daughters of those people — pumped-up, permanently training,

clean-eating behemoths — are now the mainstream. Go to any suburb or provincial town centre and you will see hordes of young men who have absorbed an aesthetic equal parts Abercrombie & Fitch and Sports Direct and mangled it into something peculiarly modern and particularly British. Zero body hair; overstyled head-hair protruding through a cap; sleeveless, loose-fitting hooded tops; flat-soled, overly technical trainers (for increased stability during deadlifts); carefully managed eyebrows; sleeve tattoos; three stone of lean muscle evenly spread over their upper torso. It's not the rotund bloat of the leather-belted bodybuilder (every town has always had a small subset of these people), this is more like a plasticated version of fighting muscle. Something that looks like it comes from MMA training, or attempting to replicate Brad Pitt's *Fight Club* physique with whatever you can buy at your local branch of GNC. It signals aggressive physicality, yet is completely unthreatening.

Sartorially, this look can be loosely traced back over the last 15 years. When American Apparel first emerged in the early noughties, their range was built around sportswear, but in a jokey, 70s-inflected, guys-like-us-wouldn't-be-seen-dead-doing-actual-sport way: tube socks, high-cut shorts, slim-fitting hoodies — and while it's hard to remember now that the company has been consumed by scandal and financial disaster, it was, briefly, a huge cultural force. Indie music's revival saw an ultra-skinny look that started as something trim and utilitarian but soon curdled into trilby-wearing hepatitis chic.

In tandem and by contrast, something harder was emerging in serious fashion shoots: early work of photographers like Alasdair McLellan, Thom Murphy's styling, and even Steven Klein's David Beckham shoot for *Arena Homme Plus* in a/w 2000 worked in an interesting area where the porny sensibility of gay-magazine culture met with something hard, provincial and ultra-straight. (A side note: in his 2011 memoir, *City Boy*, Edmund White traces the gay aesthetic of hard muscularity to the early days of the AIDS epidemic: "People who'd been fashionably skinny the year before now were beefing up to prove they weren't besieged by a wasting disease.")

In short order, a sanitised version of this look would emanate out to the mainstream (topless guys wandering around Abercrombie & Fitch; crop-haired borstal boys in trainer campaigns) and then the high street (David Gandy in his pants for M&S, fitness-supply shops in every town). And as young men in the provinces tried to emulate the look, something odd emerged — hypermasculine, straight culture dressed up in the codes and language of a *Boyz* magazine editorial from 12 years earlier. This isn't the first time that something similar has happened – think of the 70s and the yob/glam crossover with Doncaster football hooligans dressing like the bassist from The Sweet — but the incongruity is striking. Mark Simpson — the cultural commentator and journalist who first coined the term metrosexual, has christened this new look "spornosexual". "With their painstakingly pumped and chiselled bodies, muscle-enhancing tattoos, piercings, adorable beards and plunging necklines it's eye-catchingly clear that second-generation metrosexuality is less about clothes than it was for the first," he wrote in the *Telegraph*. "Eagerly self-objectifying, second-generation metrosexuality is totally tarty. Their own bodies (more than clobber and product) have become the ultimate accessories, fashioning them at the gym into a hot commodity — one that they share and compare in an online marketplace."

In public life, gym culture is now linked with the idea of a virtue. On a personal level, fitness people endlessly self-promote on Twitter and Instagram (search for the hashtag "mirin" if you want a dispiriting peek at where untrammelled vanity ends up). But a fish rots from the head down, and this kind of showboating comes from the top. David Cameron's press office regularly sets up photo opportunities of him jogging — just a few days before the general election, a *Sun* front page showed the PM clad in Lycra returning from his morning run. Think how impossible it would be to imagine a previous PM photographed in Lycra. Gordon Brown? No way. Blair? Possibly. Major, Thatcher, Ted Heath? Absolutely unthinkable. But my

hunch is that in the same way that the public now wouldn't vote for a bearded or bald man, I don't think they'd vote for an unfit one, either.

But no good deed goes unpunished and this culture isn't entirely without a dark side. Maintaining the shredded, bulked-out physique of a gym rat requires hours of daily work; young men with full-time jobs (or indeed, any jobs) don't often have that time to devote to simply cultivating their own physique. A society where a large percentage of people have sufficient free time to devote to this pursuit suggests a society that is perhaps not doing brilliantly at constructively occupying its citizens.

Of course, there are short cuts to building this kind of body. Last year the CRI charity, which runs needle exchanges, reported that it had seen a rise of almost 650 per cent in the number of steroid users between 2010 and 2013, to a point where it now outstrips heroin use. "There is a massive group of lads now, particularly in the 17 to 24 age group, that are abusing steroids something chronic, with no idea of what they're taking," one seasoned user told the BBC's *Newsbeat*. "They are messing themselves up quite severely, both mentally, hormonally and reproductively." Meanwhile, protein shakes are now stocked in supermarkets alongside regular soft drinks, just in case your protein levels need topping up during your lunch hour.

Yet if excessive gym work is a symptom of a society that has short-changed many of its young people, it's arguably also a balm of sorts. In their way, gyms function as a sort of liberal utopia. Most people realise — if only on a subconscious level — that the current system in which we live is unfair. Despite almost four decades of hyper-capitalist, free-market-dominated life becoming the norm, for most people freedom and choice is actually experienced as insecurity and exploitation. This current system has done little to make life more equitable — social mobility is decreasing, earning inequality is becoming more pronounced, and if you're dealt the wrong set of circumstances then, contrary to free-market rhetoric, your hard work won't pay off. But in the gym, it does. You're on a level playing field. There's no element of skill, or chance, or social advantage — if you go every day and lift heavy weights, you will get bigger and you will look better. There's something reassuring about it — the one place where life is actually like the way you were promised it would be when you were young and where the people who work hardest come first.

Back at the bus stop, I carry on watching the gym goers, harshly lit by the late-night strip lights, working and sweating away. In a post-religious society, it's tempting to look for substitutions for the church all over the city, but sometimes the parallels are so obvious as to be unavoidable. Beyond the big windows, light-flooded open-plan space, stirring music and Maximuscle eucharist, there's a more prosaic, social sense in which gyms might be functioning as our generation's version of places of worship. A communal space, that — at least superficially — isn't to do with shopping. A place where you can meet people from different backgrounds — and most gyms are genuinely socially and ethnically mixed in a way that few other leisure establishments are. Where you can be welcomed without judgment — even if the greeter is reading from a training manual written by the guy who used to run InterContinental Hotels — and leave after an hour feeling spiritually and psychologically better. I spend half an hour most days in the gym, and its benefits are incalculable: a ritualistic, mind-clearing, endorphin-firing experience (much of the current vogue for "mindfulness" implores you to clear thoughts from your head and focus on the moment. Believe me — if you're worrying about the imminent possibility of dropping an 80kg weight on your chest, you won't be thinking of anything else.)

The people I can see through the window look genuinely absorbed in their tasks. For that period, they are alone with their bodies, focused, self-contained. Christopher Isherwood's narrator in *A Single Man* wrote about this state. "How delightful it is to be here. If only one could spend one's entire life in this state of easygoing physical democracy." Nowadays, a lot of people can, and do.

Model: Oliver Bailey at AMCK
Make-up: Jade Bird at Frank Agency
Hair: Johnnie Biles at Frank Agency
Fashion Assistants: Sam Carder and Kamran Rajput

page 97
T-shirt, Gosha Rubchinskiy, available at Machine-A
Shorts, Nike

page 98
Shorts, Castelli, available at mrporter.com

page *100*
T-shirt, La Perla
Shorts, 2XU, available at mrporter.com
Shoes, Asics
Socks, Nike

page 103
Hoody, Champion

page 104 and 105
T-shirt, shorts, leggings, all Adidas by Kolor

Text machine

Interview by Alex Rayner

Kenneth Goldsmith doesn't write his own works, as much as copy
lines from other people. So why should we regard this self-styled
'uncreative writer' as a poetic pioneer, and why doesn't he think
anyone will read all of his new book about New York?

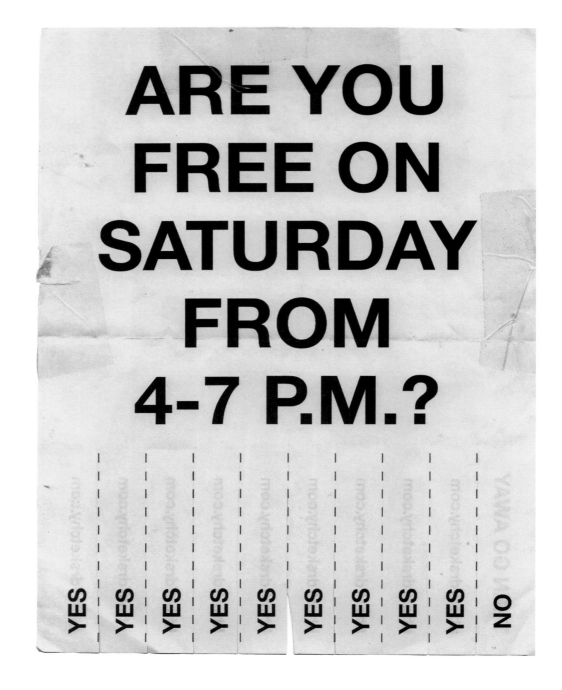

Here is a poem by the 55-year-old New York poet Kenneth Goldsmith. It is called *CCIX*, and comes from a wide-ranging collection called *No. 111.2.7.93 – 10.20.96*, published in 1997.

"My father is always looking for a solution to his many woes. This quest has led him down the New Age path. This started many years ago when he and my mother returned from a week-long Silva Mind Control seminar in Texas. Upon returning he gathered us kids into the car and told us with pride that due to the methods he had learned in the past week we would never again have to stop for a traffic light – he now could use his Mind Control to change the situation. Excitedly we climbed into the car. As we approached the first red light – voilà! – it went green. We applauded and as we came up to the next light it too turned green. Rather impressed, we awaited the next light and as we approached it it was red and it stayed that way. We stopped for that light and it looked like we'd be stopping for red lights for the foreseeable future."

Here are a few lines from a later, more famous work. This is called *The Weather* and dates from 2005:

"Well, we've got a little bit of everything here, uh, over the next forty-eight hours. Uh, at the moment, uh, we have an area of, uh, both rain and wet snow breaking out from the Pennsylvania and upstate New York, uh, some flakes have been, uh, on occasion, across Sussex and Orange County, uh, they might even pick up, uh, an inch of slushy snow there before it goes over to rain very, very late tonight. In closer to the city, we do expect to see a bit of rain at times here tonight, uh, there could be some wet snowflakes mixed in as well, at least though midnight or two in the morning, and then it's, uh, too mild aloft to support anything frozen, a low temperature of thirty-five."

You will notice a progression in style. The first piece reads like a journal entry, and describes events in Goldsmith's early life. "My parents were early New Age adopters," says the poet, who was raised in Long Island. "I grew up having to meditate, be vegetarian. I hated it. When I was old enough, all I wanted to do was sex, drugs and rock'n'roll." The second, later, extract comes from Goldsmith's "pure appropriation" period. The words were not chosen by him, at least in a conventional sense. Instead, they were transcribed from the hourly weather bulletins on 1010 WINS, a New York radio station.

Goldsmith is an "uncreative writer", to use his own term, taking words from one place and reclassing them as poetry. The poet has become famous for applying art-world practices to writing. In 2004 he began teaching a class in Uncreative Writing at the University of Pennsylvania, wherein students were awarded for skilful plagiarism and marked down for originality; in 2011 he read his work at the White House; in 2013 he became the Museum of Modern Art's first ever poet laureate. The poet acknowledges lots of fine-art influences, including Andy Warhol, John Cage and the Situationists, as

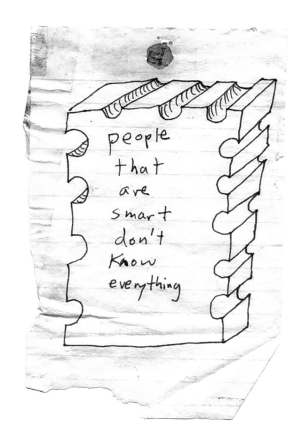

well as Allen Ginsberg and the mid-to-late 20th century New York group of writers, the Language poets. Yet, today's gallery goers might find it easier to think of him as appropriating words in the same way the Pictures Generation of painters and photographers, such as Richard Prince and Sherrie Levine, take hold of images. "I've been called the Richard Prince of poetry, for better or worse," the poet admits. "He challenged originality and creativity in the same way that I have."

Goldsmith was once a fairly straightforward fine artist. He graduated from the Rhode Island School of Design in 1984 with a BFA Sculpture, and used to show his work in New York galleries. "I was burning out on drugs," he says, recalling his first attempts at art. "I took a drawing class during my freshman year of college and I realised that art made me see the world differently. When you walked out of that class, nothing was ever the same. A car was no longer a car that got you from point A to point B. A car was something that was an amalgamation of shape and light and colour."

For a while, Goldsmith made sculptures of books. He wrote words onto the pages of these sculptures; then, in the mid-90s, he stopped sculpting and just wrote. Whereas the poetic community seemed much freer than the art world – which was, even then, heavily influenced by the art market – writers had not, in Goldsmith's view, learned from the artistic experiments of the 20th century. No one had really played around with reproducibility, as Andy Warhol had with painting; no one written a simple list of instructions for creating a literary work, as Sol LeWitt had for drawing; no one placed "found" texts in literary settings, as artists like Marcel Duchamp had with his ready-made sculptures. "Writing came to be stuck in in a pre-modernist mode," he says. "You have a few experiments with Modernism, but all writing acted like Modernism never happened. And I just really loved those experiments in art."

Goldsmith began to collect writing from a wide range of sources, not just from broadcast and print media, but via hand-made posters he found on the streets of New York. He has archived his trove, which dates back to 1985, on his Ubuweb site (ubu.com). "They're wacky, beautiful pieces of handwriting," he says of his finds. "When people have a desperate need to say something there's always a pencil and a piece of paper around." Poetry did not pay especially well, so, following his transition from visual art, Goldsmith took an office job, working for a tech start-up during the first dotcom boom. Here, by combining his fine-art theory with the labour-saving advances of the digital era, Goldsmith says he came up with an entirely new way of writing. "It blew my mind that you could copy and paste something," he recalls. "You don't realise how new that felt. I developed a whole way of writing around cut and paste."

His poem *Soliloquy* (1997) is a transcript of every word he spoke for a week; *Fidget* (2000) describes every bodily movement he made during a single

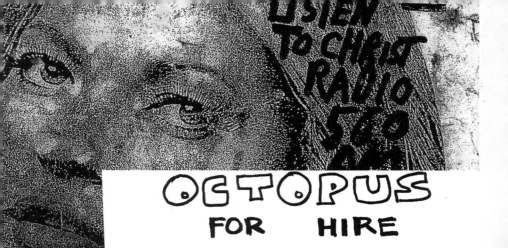

LISTEN TO CHRIST RADIO 560 AM

OCTOPUS FOR HIRE

NEED TO WHAC
SOMEBODY ??
(LOVERS, BUSINESS PARTNERS, INSURANCE FRAUD

**PROFESSIONAL, RELIABLE
LOCAL, LONG DISTANCE
LAST MINUTE**

AFFORDABLE RATES FOR EVERYBODY!!!!!

Lost my gorilla mask/
looking for a boyfriend

If found please contact:
dinhielle84@gmail.com

ALL CLO
HA

8 8 8 8 8 8 8
8 8 8 8 8 8 8
8 8 8 8 8 8 8
8 8 8 8 8 8 8
8 8 8 8 8 8 8
8 8 8 8 8 8 8
8 8 8 8 8 8 8
8 8 8 8 8 8 8
8 8 8 8 8 8 8

THIS LOOKS LIKE A GOOD PLACE TO MASTURBATE. ♥

dinhielle84@gmail.com
dinhielle84@gmail.com

l.com
ail.com
il.com
nail.com
il.com
mail.com
mail.com
mail.com
mail.com
mail.com
mail.com

FOR SALE

Self-Liposuction

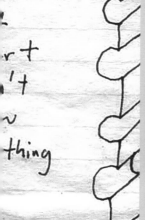

ple
t
r t
l t
thing

confess and you shall
be forgiven. (206) 376-7459

Often when I day

I just create scenarios

my head of the two

www.TrueArtisForRebels.com

Your Glasses Broke on this corner. Call me:

212-579-3119

...ATION APPRECIATED —
WOULD YOU LIKE TO DONATE A TRILLION I CAN TRY TO GE... A LIFE

MINDLESS SELF INDULGENCE
NEEDS A FUCKING DRUMMER.
IF YOU ARE A GIRL OR A
BOY BETWEEN THE AGES OF
18-27 AND LIKE TO HIT STUFF
YOU MAY BE ELIGIBLE TO BE
OUR YOUNG FRESH SUCKER IF
YOU CALL THIS NUMBER
(212) 266-5822
YOU HAD BETTER BE YOUNG
COOL AND STYLEISH AND NOT
BE WASTING MY MOTHER FUCKING
TIME SO CALL IF YOU LIKE
SEX PISTOLS NIN OLD SCHOOL
RAP JUNGLE YOUR MOTHERS
SMELLY ASS AND YOU DONT
MIND DRUMMING FOR A BAND OF

PEOPLE WHO DON'T RECYCLE SHOULD BE BRUTALLY EATEN. ♥

HOSPITAL WEEK 5/9 - 5/12
SIGN UP VOL. OFFICE 392B.

HULA HOOP CONTEST MAY 12

FIRE

I LOST MY FAVORITE STUFFED ANIMAL. IF YOU FOUND HIM, PLEASE CALL 718-399-6344

I'LL PROBABLY NEVER GO THERE!!!!
"it seems to me"...

day; in *Day* (2003) he retyped every line from a single daily edition of the *New York Times*; *Traffic* (2007) consists of transcribed traffic reports; *Sports* (2008) is the commentary from a New York Yankees game. Who actually reads these poems? Well, Goldsmith prefers to think of his audience as a "thinkership", rather than a readership, and admits that it is sometimes better to talk about his books "rather than read them in a traditional way".

If you find this all a little hard to bear, you're far from alone. Many poets and general readers have objected to Goldsmith's innovations. Goldsmith himself is not sure why he irritates people, though in most cases he believes that "they haven't read the texts. People are really quick to judge something they know nothing about." Some argue that his "uncreative" techniques dehumanise the act of writing, though Goldsmith denies this, defending, for example, his *Day*, *Traffic* and *Sports* series as highly personal works, evocative of New York, his home town. "Everything I do is very humanist," he says. "All my work is full of the traditional content writing has always had, it's just that sometimes I don't generate it, I select it."

In Goldsmith's view, it is the literary community that is not acknowledging the true state of humanity in the 21st century. Just as in 1936 the German cultural critic Walter Benjamin suggested that the role of the artist changed with the arrival of photography and other forms of mechanical reproduction, so Goldsmith argues that the role of the writer has altered with the rise of the internet. Words, like pictures, are now much more easy to copy, repurpose and reproduce.

This comparison isn't absolute. You can't click a button to "write" a text description of Wordsworth's bank of daffodils, as a camera could capture some aspects of a scene quicker and better than a painter could. However you can, as Goldsmith points out, "find plenty of descriptions on the web and just cut and paste them." He says, "I could find 10 of them, and I could mash them together and get the perfect description of a bank of daffodils."

In Goldsmith's view, outdated ideas of authorship, copyright and literary tradition will all be swept away by this deluge of text, in the same way that pre-modern ideas of art and the artist have been eroded over the past century and a half. "To me it's an inevitability," he says. "The digital era is with us. You can hold onto your pre-digital ideas, but the world is moving. I think everyone will find that there is still room for expression and creativity; we just have to think about it a little differently in the 21st century, that's all."

Authorial appropriation has its limits. In March of this year Goldsmith received a great deal of criticism following a reading at Brown University in Rhode Island. The four-day event, called Interrupt 3, described itself as a "discussion forum and studio for new forms of language art". On 13 March, Goldsmith read *The Body of Michael Brown*, a reworking of the autopsy report published following the death of the unarmed African-American teenager, who was shot by a police officer in Ferguson, Missouri.

Many found a privileged white man's appropriation of this particular text – which Goldsmith rewrote slightly and reordered, ending his poem with the autopsy's description of the boy's penis – incredibly distasteful. Cathy Park Hong, the poetry editor of the *New Republic* said that Goldsmith had "reached new racist lows"; Goldsmith himself asked the university not to post the recording of his piece online and today admits the whole thing was "a mistake". "If I knew then what I know now I never would have done that piece," Goldsmith says. "My poem set out to be a protest piece, to show the violence that those 11 bullets did to a perfectly normal, beautiful body. However, I wasn't aware that it wasn't my place to perform that poem. I've come to realise that over the past six months."

He is surer about his 913-page new book. *Capital* is a huge collection of quotations about New York in the 20th century. Organised under rubrics including "unrest", "sex", "dirt" and "downtown", as well as "Coney Island", "Harlem" and "Central Park", it is a homage to Walter Benjamin's Arcades Project, an equally massive collection of citations about life in Paris, which Benjamin left unfinished on his death in 1940.

FASHION = FASCISM

The book took Goldsmith 10 years to write – if "write" is the correct verb here, as there's barely a line of his own text in it. Instead, its content varies from pithy quotes like "Gum holds subway doors together" taken from Gay Talese's book *New York: A Serendipiter's Journey* (1961), through to far longer passages from other sources – including newspapers, screenplays, magazines, novels and academic papers – taking in such subjects as the photographer Robert Mapplethorpe, the urban planner Robert Moses and the 1939 and 1964 World's Fairs. The earliest quote dates from New Year's Eve 1899; the most recent is from 10 September 2001.

It is also a pleasant read, even if readers are unlikely to progress from the first page through to the end. Goldsmith himself doubts anyone will read the whole thing. He also believes that the city in his book is quite different from the New York of today. "I'd walk out of a library having been researching the book, into Greenwich Village 2014, and I couldn't find any of the 20th century that I had been reading about there," he says. "Well, the buildings are there, but nothing else." Today's New York, in Goldsmith's view, is a wealthier, more globalist and more protected city. There's a melancholic note to his voice when he says this, though he denies he misses the city of his youth. "New York is a great place because it keeps changing. Sometimes it changes in ways that you don't like, but if you aren't willing to go for the ride, then New York is really not the place for you."

Paris was the capital of the art world during the 19th century, just as New York was the capital in the 20th century. If someone were to write a similar Arcades Project for the 21st century, where might this be based? Goldsmith thinks about this for less than a second. "Probably the internet," he replies. "Yeah," more definitely, "I'd say the internet."

PLEASE

ENOUGH with the TATTOOS, LOGOS, PIERCINGS, SKULL + CAMO WEAR. Your cliché-ridden fashion (non) sense is pathetic + *extremely* conformist.

PLEASE, DON'T TAKE ME INTO ANOTHER GALLERY.

NOTICE

Chuck Close's 15 minutes of fame have officially expired.

All street posters from Kenneth Goldsmith's archive.
1985 to present. ubu.com

Two years on from her death, more and more viewers appreciate
the enduring power of Deborah Turbeville's images. As the Foxy
Production gallery in New York prepares to open a new show of

Deborah Turbeville's photographs broke all the rules of fashion photography when they first graced the pages of *Vogue* in the 1970s; her shots of sullen models in derelict settings were dark, sometimes out of focus, with the emphasis decidedly not on the clothing. She went so far as to scratch and puncture her negatives, toying with the physical medium of the photograph as she updated one of its favourite subjects (beautiful women) for a new era. Far from images of idealised Venuses performing for men while selling women's clothing, Turbeville's subtle, complex representations of femininity helped to shift fashion photography into a more explicitly artistic idiom. The influence of her innovations is still being felt today, years after her death in 2013.

Her work is now the subject of an exhibition at Foxy Production, a contemporary art gallery located in Manhattan's Chelsea neighbourhood. The show, which runs until 17 October, features works from her Rainy Day People series, commissioned by *L'Uomo Vogue* in 1995 and shot in Lancaster, Massachusetts, not far from where she grew up in Stoneham, MA. I sat down with the gallery's co-founder and director John Thomson, and Mary Barone, the New York writer, photographer and friend of Turbeville, to discuss the legacy and continuing significance of this giant of contemporary photography. The following transcript has been edited and condensed for clarity. *Dylan Kerr, Brooklyn, New York, August 2015*

Above: Bathhouse, 1975
Courtesy the Estate of Deborah Turbeville,
New York and Foxy Production, New York

All other images: Rainy Day People, 1995
Courtesy the Estate of Deborah Turbeville,
New York and Foxy Production, New York

Dylan Kerr: *It's hard to reckon with the impact Turbeville's photographs had when she began her career in the 1970s, in part because her subdued, gritty tone has now been so fully subsumed into contemporary fashion photography. What kinds of reactions did these images generate in the 70s?*

Mary Barone: In 1975, when *Vogue* published The Bathhouse series, they were shocking. I was a teenager then, and they left a big impression on me — on any woman, I think, that saw that body of work when it was published.

In the analogue days of the 70s, we got our information about the world — especially its more erotic aspects — from these magazines. Deborah's images were especially captivating because they employed that eroticism in an entirely different way than something like *Playboy*. I think her work is usually thought of in terms of the avant-garde or its eroticism, but I don't think it has been properly examined for what it's really about, which is women and their private spaces — both psychological and physical.

John Thomson: She was embedding in her photographs a whole lot of different levels that were not in fashion photography before her. There was high style, with [German-American photographer Horst P] Horst and those types, but she really went on a completely different track to that. It wasn't the glorified, idealised woman. It was a group of detached yet feisty women, all together but not looking at each other. What was their connection? It was a real departure.

DK: *Turbeville is considered a major innovator of fashion photography in the 20th century, alongside Helmut* Newton and Guy Bourdin, *but her work seems relatively overlooked by the wider public. Why do you think that is?*

JT: That's a hard question to answer, because people who are in the know about fashion photography wouldn't think she's been overlooked. With that said, Bourdin and Newton have had huge museum shows across the world and she just hasn't had as much exposure. People get rediscovered and repositioned at different times during their career and after their passing. It's hard to predict how a career will change or be received.

MB: Those three were really the triumvirate. I think a lot of it has to do with publishing, and the kinds of images they worked with. Helmut Newton published a lot of books with his big shots of nude women, but I don't think Deborah really wanted that for herself.

DK: *Turbeville certainly portrayed women in an entirely different register than her male counterparts. Looking back at her work, can we read Turbeville as a feminist artist?*

MB: I don't know if she was a bra-burning feminist in the 70s, but she was a woman who was living and working during that period. It's naturally going to affect her creative sensibility. She was clearly defying the way the culture was taught to look at women.

JT: There's obviously a long history of the male gaze in photography, but women photographing women in a sexualised position is a very different and interesting thing altogether. She helped to change the way women are imaged in fashion photography, to really undermine the tenets of how it was traditionally done. Her work is political, even if she wasn't necessarily thinking about that at the time. I see her as both an artist and a great fashion photographer. She was given the opportunity to release her artistic impulses through commissions from fashion magazines, and she really found a way to express herself.

DK: *Turbeville's work is usually considered in the context of fashion rather than fine art. How does her work function in the gallery setting?*

JT: Many people who do commercial photography have this other space where they do their artwork. There's a division. With Deborah, I think that there wasn't that dichotomy between these two things. Her commercial work had all of her artistic drive. She wasn't holding back — it was all there in her work.

MB: She was using fashion as the medium for her creativity. She didn't care that she was selling clothes. In some of these shots, she didn't even put the clothes on the models. She wanted to create something different for herself.

DK: *What can contemporary photographers learn from looking at Turbeville's work and career?*

MB: I would say the freedom that she maintained over her own image making is her most important attribute. That's what makes her and her work exciting. She explored her own aesthetic so deeply and with such intensity — her photographs are so free of any other protocol. I think looking at Deborah Turbeville's work — and realising that she showed it in *Vogue* — gives people permission to assert their own vision. *foxyproduction.com*

Patterns of consumption

Interview by Alex Rayner

**On the eve of her new London exhibition,
we speak to the American painter
Katherine Bernhardt about Moroccan
carpets, Kate Moss and coffee**

You can spot the Pop Art influences in Katherine Bernhardt's paintings pretty easily. She first found fame seven or eight years ago with her angular, slapdash depictions of fashion models, and, more recently began filling her canvases featuring a wider range of objects, from hammerhead sharks through to headphones, Chapsticks, Swatch watches and basketballs. Yet, unlike, Warhol, there's no cool comment on the reproducibility of images here, or knowing exaltation of the beauty in commerce in her work.

The 40-year-old artist's free, fast style of painting brings to mind the brushwork of German Abstract- and Neo-Expressionism. However, Bernhardt dodges the sombre angst often dwelt on by those predecessors.

Her repeated motifs, as she explains below, draw from the anti-minimalist, worldly, vernacular artistry of the late-20th century Pattern and Decoration movement, which sought to undermine the solemn, white males who once dominated fine art. Only, Bernhardt's paintings also look too jolly, lascivious and downright good to be tied up with these slightly outdated concerns.

The artist was born in Missouri, married a Moroccan man whom she met on a rug-buying trip to Essaouira, and now lives in New York, painting pictures that appear to cycle through different enthusiasms, be they tropical fruit, cigarettes or consumer durables. In this way she seems to capture all the bright, silly, covetable goods we end up wanting these days, when no overarching art movement holds sway, and instead, an unending stream of goods and opportunities passes before our eyes.

Alex Rayner: *Could you tell us about Mr Coffee?*

Katherine Bernhardt: Mr Coffee is an amazing machine that brews my coffee every morning.

AR: *Do you tend to like or dislike the objects you paint?*

KB: I tend to like them. I don't think I would paint something I didn't like. I would have no interest in it at all.

AR: *In the past you have referenced consumerist items like Swatch watches and burgers, as well as found objects from other cultures, like north African rugs. Do these objects serve an intellectual purpose within your work, or are they primarily items that you have reacted to on a more instinctive or aesthetic level?*

KB: Both. The items represent American culture, pop culture, and relate to Andy Warhol and Philip Guston and Henri Matisse in the way that they are painted. The items are also shapes in themselves that work as shapes of an abstract object pattern painting.

AR: *When you paint models are you working with life models or from photographs? And does it matter in terms of your relationship to the subject?*

KB: I was working from torn-out magazine photos from *Elle* and *Vogue*. I've never met any of the models. It's more about obsession, or the things that I'm obsessed with: Moroccan carpets, Kate Moss or coffee.

AR: *You've said in the past that you tend to complete a painting quite quickly. Is this still so? How do you know when one is finished?*

KB: I do work fast. It's immediate and fresh. Knowing if a painting is finished is an instinct, I guess.

AR: *Can you give us some further insight into the way you work? You've said that you paint quickly, but how about your research period? Do you research each painting specifically or do you tend to hoard visual references as you go along?*

KB: I hoard visual references in my head. I also take pictures of delis and posters in delis or 99-cent stores. I work spontaneously, so I just think of things I want in a painting and then do it. I draw it out first in spray paint and paint it on the floor. That way it can be very liquidy.

AR: *Do you like to hang on to your paintings for a while before they go on display? Does your view of them change over time?*

KB: It's good to be able to see your paintings for a while in the studio and also to have people see them and critique them. Some of the ones that I hate other people love; it's their favourite. Other ones that I love, people have no interest in.

AR: *Quite a few commentators describe your painting style as combining Pop Art and Expressionism — two styles that are often seen as being in opposition to one another. Is this an accurate characterisation?*

KB: Painting now can be a mix of anything and any style, but you have to make it your own somehow. I see my work more as influenced by [1970s and 80s US art movement] Pattern and Decoration, or related to Paul Gauguin or Henri Matisse.

AR: *Do you feel like you're part of any wider network, or is there any one artist at the moment whose art you feel a connection with? Isn't all art a reaction to other people's art?*

KB: It's a dialogue related to all other contemporary art and art that came before it.

AR: *Which other painters do you admire?*

KB: Matisse, Peter Doig, Chris Ofili, Laura Owens.

AR: *Other painters' work aside, what else do you find visually exciting or engaging at the moment?*

KB: Hand-painted murals and hand-painted signs.

AR: *Are there any common misunderstandings when it comes to your paintings? Or anything that is often overlooked?*

KB: Lots of people like to say, "Oh, my child could have painted that. It looks like a kid did it." These people are haters. Actually, I just make it look easy. Try making it yourself before judging. I dare you.

Katherine Bernhardt's exhibition is on from 12 October to 14 November 2015 at the Carl Freedman Gallery, 29 Charlotte Road, London EC2A 3PB
carlfreedman.com

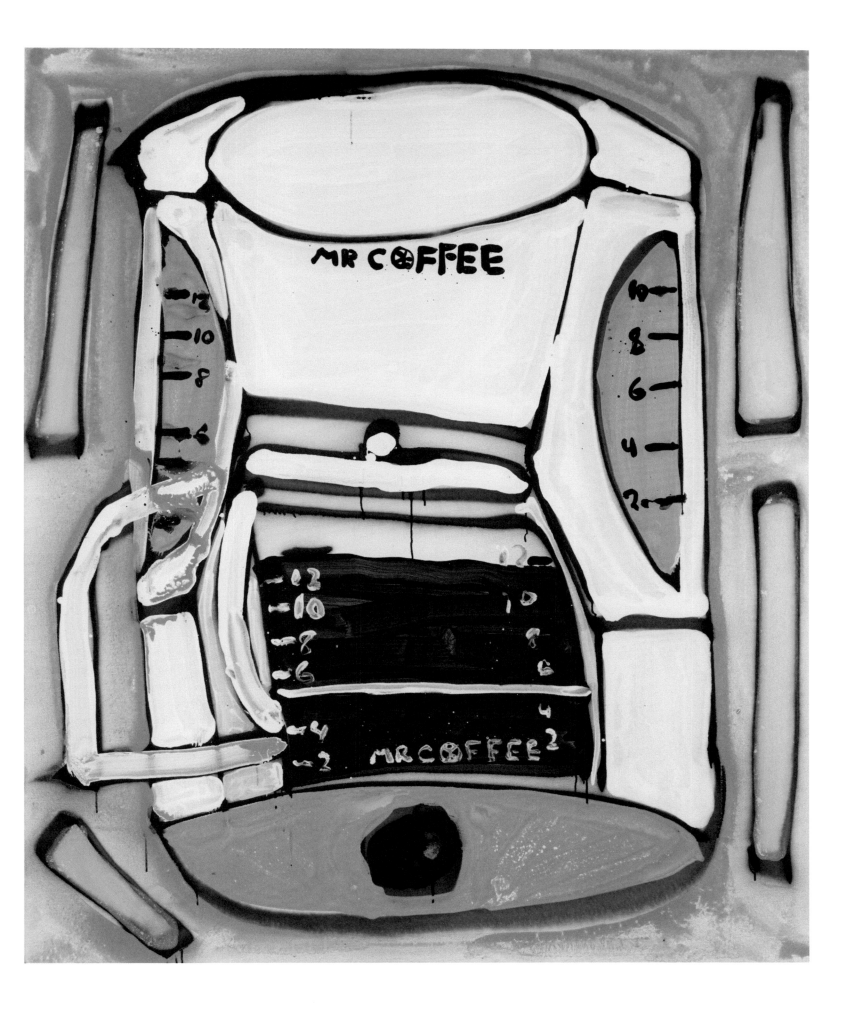

Mr. Coffee and French Fries, 2015
© Katherine Bernhardt
Courtesy of Carl Freedman Gallery

IL TEMPO PASSA

BRUCE ROGERS

Supplement is set in the Centaur typeface, first created a little over 100 years ago by the brilliant US typographer, and, perhaps, the first great professional book designer, Bruce Rogers. Rogers was born in Indiana in 1870, studied art at university and worked as a fine book designer, first in Boston then, in 1912, in New York City, where he was employed by the Metropolitan Museum of Art.

Although he arrived in NYC, the metropolis of the 20th century art world, at the very beginning of the Modernist era, Rogers favoured orderliness over experimentation. He based his Centaur letters on the work of 15th century French print designer and engraver Nicolas Jenson, who is widely credited with creating one of the earliest and most elegant Roman typefaces.

Rogers first employed Centaur in a privately pressed English translation of the French poet Maurice de Guérin's whimsical mythical work, *The Centaur*. The typeface takes its title from this initial appearance, as was the tradition at that time. The Met sponsored Rogers' designs and, in 1914 used the upper-case version of Centaur for its signage. He went on to work in Britain for extended periods, using Centaur in a 1932 translation of Homer's *The Odyssey* by TE Lawrence, and in 1935, for his Oxford Lectern Bible, which is widely regarded as the designer's masterpiece.

The type foundry Monotype commissioned a commercially available edition of Centaur from Rogers, which was released in 1929. It is now being updated by the firm, ensuring that Rogers' century-old script with a renaissance pedigree finds new uses within the work of today's designers.